D0897989

One Bloody Thing After Another

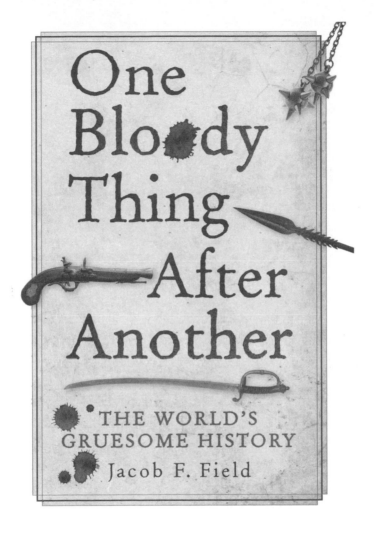

One Bloody Thing After Another

THE WORLD'S GRUESOME HISTORY

Jacob F. Field

Michael O'Mara Books Limited

First published in Great Britain in 2012 by
Michael O'Mara Books Limited
9 Lion Yard
Tremadoc Road
London SW4 7NQ

A CIP catalogue record for this book is available from the British Library.

Papers used by Michael O'Mara Books Limited are natural, recyclable
products made from wood grown in sustainable forests. The manufacturing
processes conform to the environmental regulations of the country of origin.

ISBN: 978-1-84317-884-2 in hardback print format
ISBN: 978-1-84317-918-4 in EPub format
ISBN: 978-1-84317-917-7 in Mobipocket format

1 2 3 4 5 6 7 8 9 10

www.mombooks.com

Designed and typeset by K DESIGN, Winscombe, Somerset
Jacket design by Ana Bježančević
Maps by David Woodroffe
Picture on p. 146: Morphart Creations Inc./www.shutterstock.com

Printed and bound in Great Britain by Clays Ltd, St Ives plc

Contents

Foreword

Foreword

VIOLENCE, TORTURE, MASSACRE, tyranny and disaster litter the annals of world history. Accompanying the most important junctures through time are mayhem and madness, battles and bloodshed. This book uncovers the gruesome behind the great, and the repugnant behind the powerful, all the while sticking to the facts. History really is this bloody.

Emperors and kings were often wholly unsuitable to rule their people – indeed, were even a danger to them. King Charles VI of France's frequent bouts of madness dangerously destabilized his kingdom during the Hundred Years' War, allowing England to conquer large swathes of France. The eighteenth-century Korean prince Sado was considered such a menace that he was sentenced to death by being sealed into a chest for eight days. Other rulers, like Queen Ranavalona of Madagascar or Tsar Ivan the Terrible of Russia, were virtually psychotic, wantonly executing thousands of their subjects.

Historic rulers were not reluctant to use sadistic and esoteric methods of punishment and execution; from the tyrant Perillos's brazen bull, to the ancient Persian practice of scaphism, history shows us there is no limit to human cruelty. The onset of new regimes and dynasties usually meant uncompromising purges of potential opponents. From the ancient Roman emperor Caracalla to the seventeenth-century Shah of Persia, Safi I, new rulers frequently instituted their reigns with bloodshed.

Wars and battles are a constant presence in world history. Seldom were any fought fairly and often they descended into brutal massacres of both soldiers and civilians, such as at the sackings of Yangzhou, Magdeburg or Drogheda. Heroic rebels often did not triumph in the face of adversity. Rather, like the Scottish patriot William Wallace, they were punished. When revolts and rebellions did succeed the new regimes were often more bloody than those they replaced. In the aftermath of the French Revolution, the Reign of Terror saw tens of thousands guillotined.

Looming over all of man's mayhem was the constant spectre of disastrous events such as earthquakes, pestilence and famine. Over 50,000 were killed when a major earthquake struck Lisbon in 1755, while a 1657 fire that devastated Tokyo led to the deaths of almost 100,000. The failure of the potato harvest in mid-nineteenth-century Ireland virtually halved the island's population. But perhaps the most devastating disaster was the medieval Black Death, where plague wiped out one-third of Europe's population.

History is rarely the sanitized litany of dates and events it sometimes appears to be in textbooks. *One Bloody Thing After Another* details chronologically the most gruesome of these moments over 3,000 years, from the dissolute King Shou of Shang in eleventh-century BC China to King Leopold II's horrific exploitation of the Congo during the late-nineteenth century. Covering every inhabited continent, this book explores how history can literally be one bloody thing after another.

Jacob F. Field, 2012

The
Ancient World

c.1000 BC to AD 500

KING SHOU OF SHANG

THE LAST OF the Shang Dynasty of Chinese kings, Shou ruled between 1075 and 1046 BC. From his splendid capital city of Yin, Shou's immorality and cruelty knew no limits. He wholly ignored matters of state, with the exception of setting extremely high taxes to fund his debauched lifestyle. Drunken orgies were commonplace at court. One of Shou's most infamous follies was constructing a large pool, filled with wine and overhanging with branches of roasted meat. Shou and his companions could then float on the pool in canoes, reaching down to drink and up to eat. His favourite concubine was Daji, for whom he built pleasure gardens filled with rare and exotic creatures – all at the expense of his downtrodden subjects.

Depiction of a man being flayed alive

THE END OF A DYNASTY

Punishments for anyone who dared speak against Shou were profoundly cruel. One court official was flayed alive, while another was carved into strips and hung out like dried meat. Shou's own uncle was put to death by having his heart plucked out. A favourite form of execution was to warm a metal cylinder until red-hot and force the condemned to embrace it.

The reign of terror came to an end when an army supporting the rebel leader Wu of the Zhou Dynasty defeated Shou's army at the battle of Muye. Knowing that the end of his regime was inevitable, Shou retreated to his burning palace and committed suicide. The new king, Wu, placed Shou's head on a stake outside Yin's gates for all to see.

KING ASHURBANIPAL OF ASSYRIA

Ashurbanipal, who reigned from 668 to 627 BC, was the last great king of the Neo-Assyrian Empire, which spread across the Middle East and into parts of North Africa and Anatolia. Although famed for building a vast library at Nineveh, Ashurbanipal's cruelty was more renowned. His armies laid waste to the lands of his enemies, destroying towns, smashing dams, and setting crops alight. He was brutal to captives, severing their hands, noses, ears and fingers. When one of his cities rebelled, he slaughtered its people and piled the corpses in front of the main gate. Rebellious nobles were flayed and their skins hung over the city walls.

THE BRAZEN BULL

Phalaris, a Greek tyrant ruler of Agrigentum in Sicily, seized power in around 570 BC and extended his rule over much of the island. He was rumoured to be a cannibal who devoured infant children, but his cruellest legacy was the brazen bull, which he commissioned to be the means of execution for capital crimes. Invented by Perillos of Athens, the device itself was simple – a hollow bronze bull with a door in its side. Its application, however, was horrific. The condemned was placed inside the bull and a fire was lit below; as it became red-hot, it roasted the victim. Ingeniously, the device converted the smoke produced by the burning human into clouds of incense. A further refinement was a system of pipes and stops in the bull's head, which made the victim's screams sound like a bellowing bull.

When he first revealed his contraption, Perillos offered to display this feature by climbing inside. Cruel Phalaris ordered that the door be locked and a fire set beneath the device. Perillos's screams did indeed turn into a bull's bellows, but he was pulled out before it was too late. Rather than receive a reward or fee for his invention, Perillos was thrown to his death from a hilltop. The writer Lucian of Samosata claimed that Phalaris reacted so harshly to the inventor because even he 'loathed the thought of such ingenious cruelty', and vowed to punish its creator.

Ironically, it was the bull that killed Phalaris when he was overthrown around twenty years later: a mob seized him and bundled him inside Perillos's invention where he was roasted alive.

A victim is placed inside the brazen bull

THE EXECUTION OF MITHRIDATES

The revolt of Cyrus the Younger against his elder brother King Artaxerxes II of Persia ended at the battle of Cunaxa in 401 BC. A soldier named Mithridates had struck Cyrus in the temple with a spear, dazing him. As Cyrus shakily remounted his horse, another soldier struck his leg. In this diminished state, Cyrus fell from his animal and died as his wounded temple hit the ground.

A proud man, Artaxerxes wanted it believed he had killed Cyrus with his own hand. Mithridates was showered with costly gifts with the proviso he allow Artaxerxes to take credit for the death of his brother. But Mithridates, drunk on wine, bragged of his achievement at a banquet after the battle. So incensed was Artaxerxes that his lies had been revealed, he ordered Mithridates to be put to death by scaphism, also known as 'the torture of the boats'.

The process was savage. The victim was confined between two narrow boats (or hollow tree trunks), which fully enclosed his body but left his hands, head and feet protruding. He was then force-fed a mixture of milk and honey, which was also poured over his face to draw flies and other insects. Eventually the boats would fill up with the excrement of the victim, who was periodically fed with more milk and honey to keep him alive for as long as possible. Over time, gangrene would take hold in the victim's extremities. The build-up of faeces attracted maggots, which would breed in the body and slowly consume the victim's flesh.

The historian Plutarch records that Mithridates was subjected to this agonizing torture for seventeen days before he died. Artaxerxes remained king for another forty-three years.

THE CONQUEST OF KALINGA

Ashoka the Great had carved out an empire that covered most of the Indian subcontinent. One of the last areas to hold out against him was Kalinga, a kingdom on India's east coast. In 265 BC, Ashoka attacked with an army of 400,000 – vastly outnumbering his enemy. Aided by battle elephants, Kalinga valiantly struggled, but this only provoked Ashoka's army to commit numerous acts of brutality against the population, killing over 100,000 civilians. In one particularly bloody episode, the waters of the Daya River ran red with blood. Kalinga was left ruined.

Left appalled by the vile destruction he had sanctioned, Ashoka converted to Buddhism and forswore violence for ever.

THE FIRST EMPEROR OF CHINA

Qin Shi Huang became the first emperor of a unified China in 221 BC. He reformed the country, established the Great Wall, and constructed his massive tomb at Xi'an, guarded by thousands of life-sized terracotta soldiers. To achieve this undoubted greatness, Qin's rule was ruthless and proscriptive. Infamously, in 213 BC, Qin ordered that all books be destroyed in order to forestall any criticism of his regime by comparison with those of the past. The only volumes saved from the flames were works on medicine, divination, agriculture and the history of his dynasty. Any who dared to mention old records were publicly executed, and the families of those critical of Qin's rule were obliterated. Citizens found in possession of proscribed works had their faces tattooed and were condemned to labour on the Great Wall. When a group of scholars continued to speak out against the emperor they were put on trial – 460 were buried alive.

QIN'S SEARCH FOR IMMORTALITY

As he grew older, Qin became obsessed with finding the elixir of life. The greatest scholars in China were set to work on creating a potion of immortality. Some of those who failed were executed. Qin became increasingly reclusive, shutting himself away from cares of state and avoiding contact with his people by moving between his various residences via a network of tunnels. Qin died in 211 BC as a result of mercury poisoning. Ironically, he had been ingesting the element believing it would grant him eternal life.

SPARTA

Renowned for its military pre-eminence, Sparta's rigorous society focused on excellence. In this, the most martial of the ancient Greek city states, infants were examined at birth and the weak or deformed were thrown from the cliffs. From the age of eight, children were given stringent military training, housed in dormitories and provided with meagre rations. While they were encouraged to steal food, if they were caught they received a public beating. As a result of this brutal instruction the Spartan army was the lynchpin of the Greek forces that pushed back the Persians in the fifth century BC. However, by the end of the third century BC, Spartan potency had begun to fade.

THE TYRANT KING OF SPARTA

Sparta's last independent ruler was Nabis, who seized power in 207 BC. He embarked on a lengthy series of reforms, freeing slaves and redistributing the land and property of the wealthy and noble to the people. Anyone who fled Sparta was hunted down and killed or brought back to face Nabis. Those who opposed him faced a torture device called the Apega of Nabis, similar to the iron maiden. The machine was a replica of his wife Apega and worked by 'embracing' the victim with its arms, pressing him or her close. The historian Polybius recorded that its breasts, hands, and arms were studded with iron spikes, which could be controlled with secret springs and switches. Nabis used the device to slowly crush his enemies until they submitted to his will. He was overthrown in 192 BC, and Sparta became part of the Achaean League.

THE PHARAOH WHO MURDERED HIS WIFE AND LOST HIS LIFE

By the first century BC, the pharaohs had progressively shrunk in influence to become virtual clients of the Roman Republic. In 80 BC, Ptolemy IX died, leaving his daughter Berenice III as queen. Sulla, the dictator of Rome, sent his protégé Ptolemy XI to Egypt to marry Berenice and act as a pro-Roman influence. The young man was to rule jointly with Berenice, both his stepmother and half-sister, who some also believed to be his natural mother. Berenice, however, was reluctant to cede any power to her new husband. Stung by this, Ptolemy XI arranged for her murder after only nineteen days of marriage. The citizens of Alexandria were enraged and he was promptly lynched, dragged from his palace and beaten to death.

SLAVERY AND REBELLION

In ancient Rome slaves were subject to brutal punishments at the whim of their owners. Flogging was commonplace. Those who attempted to escape and were caught were branded on the forehead. Some were punished by being suspended from their hands with weights attached to their feet until they were at the point of death. When slaves were sentenced to death, crucifixion was the most common means of execution. Whipped and beaten, the condemned slaves were marched to the place of execution wearing a *furca*, a heavy V-shaped metal collar, which was fixed over the back of the neck, and with their hands bound to their thighs. In the fourth century AD, under Emperor Constantine I, slaves found guilty of seduction were executed by having molten lead poured down their throats. Perhaps as a result of this treatment there were three major slave uprisings between 135 and 71 BC, the last and greatest of which was the revolt led by Spartacus.

THE END OF SPARTACUS'S REVOLT

Spartacus was a former gladiator from Thrace (which covered parts of what is now Bulgaria, Greece, and Turkey) who escaped from his master in 73 BC and quickly gained a following of fellow escapees. He crushed all forces sent against him until 71 BC, when a force of Roman legions finally defeated him. Spartacus was wounded in the thigh by a spear, and then overwhelmed by a great mass of legionaries. His body was never recovered. The 6,000 slaves who survived the battle were captured by the Romans and crucified along the 120 miles of the Appian Way that ran between Rome and Capua. Their decaying bodies were left as a warning to any slaves who might consider revolt.

THE BLOODY END OF THE ROMAN REPUBLIC

On 10 January 49 BC, Julius Caesar and his army crossed the Rubicon River, the border between the province of Cisalpine Gaul and Italy proper. Entering Italy was forbidden, as the troops could be used to seize power in Rome. This, however, was exactly what Caesar intended, and his action ignited nearly two decades of bloody conflict that saw the establishment of the Roman Empire at the expense of the Republic.

THE TRIUMPH AND DEATH OF JULIUS CAESAR

As Caesar marched on Rome, his opposition, made up of senators who believed he had grown too powerful, retreated south to Capua, leaving the capital defenceless. Caesar's enemies in the civil war were led by his erstwhile ally, Pompey, who fled across the Mediterranean, pursued by Caesar's forces. In 48 BC, Pompey docked in Egypt. Its ruler Ptolemy XIII sent a small boat to fetch Pompey from his galley. As his supporters and family looked on, Pompey was rowed to shore to what he believed was a meeting with Ptolemy. However, hoping to curry Caesar's favour in his dynastic struggle with his sister Cleopatra VII, Ptolemy had ordered his henchmen to murder Pompey. He called for the severed head to be displayed to Caesar.

The plan backfired spectacularly. When Caesar arrived in Egypt he was appalled and backed Cleopatra, with whom he began an affair that bore him a son, Caesarion, in 47 BC. Caesar returned to Rome in triumph. To celebrate he held spectacular games, using the Circus Maximus to host a battle to the death between two armies of 500 war captives, 20 elephants, and 40 horsemen.

Meanwhile, however, there was increasing senatorial opposition to Caesar's dictatorial rule, and a plot was forged to assassinate him. On the 15 March 44 BC (the 'Ides of March'), a group surprised Caesar as he took his seat in the Senate. Caesar attempted in vain to defend himself with a stylus – he was stabbed twenty-three times and died on the Senate floor.

THE BEGINNING OF THE ROMAN EMPIRE

In the aftermath of Caesar's assassination, Mark Antony, Caesar's most trusted deputy, and Octavian, Caesar's legal heir and grand-nephew, rose to become the most important leaders in Rome. After Antony's wife died, he married Octavian's sister in 40 BC. However, tensions simmered between him and Octavian, exacerbated by Antony's affair with Cleopatra, and by 31 BC they were at war. Octavian quickly crushed his foe, and Antony was forced to flee to Egypt. As Octavian approached Alexandria in August 30 BC, Antony's men deserted en masse. Defeat was inevitable for Antony and Cleopatra. In August 30 BC, Antony stabbed himself with a sword, believing that his lover had also committed suicide, and Octavian's men took control of Alexandria.

Cleopatra was trapped. She did not want to be paraded through Rome in chains and so committed suicide. It is improbable she used a cobra, as is popularly believed, but would have sought a more reliable route to death, such as hemlock or a toxic ointment. Eventually Cleopatra's corpse was discovered, dressed in full royal regalia, next to her two chief handmaids. Cleopatra's son Caesarion was proclaimed pharaoh, but Octavian had him killed. He was the last of the pharaohs, and on his death Egypt became a province of Rome. Octavian, who renamed himself Augustus in 27 BC, went on to be the first Emperor of Rome and ruled until his death in 14 BC.

EMPEROR CALIGULA

Between AD 37 and 41, ancient Rome had one of its cruellest rulers. Bloodshed and tyranny were the hallmarks of Caligula's reign.

THE EDUCATION OF A TYRANT

In AD 31, Caligula went to live with his great-uncle, Emperor Tiberius. Tiberius's estate on the island of Capri was a den of perversion and iniquity. The palace was filled with erotic paintings and sculptures to inspire the trained teams of sexual performers who staged orgies for the emperor's pleasure. Tiberius delighted in innovative methods of torture, inventing a form in which the victims were plied with copious amounts of wine, and then tied up in such a way as to prevent them from relieving themselves. Rome welcomed Tiberius's death, but his successor would prove to be no more humane. According to the historian Cassius Dio, Caligula 'not only emulated but even surpassed his predecessor's licentiousness and bloodthirstiness'.

ENTERTAINMENTS FIT FOR AN EMPEROR

Caligula's first years as emperor were moderate, and he was popular with the people of Rome. This was not to last. Over time, he became more and more obsessed with grand public spectacles, even taking part himself – driving chariots, fighting as a gladiator, and acting on the stage. Caligula's games were cruel, even by the standards of the time. Prisoners were thrown to wild beasts, but not before their tongues were gouged out to prevent them from screaming. When animal feed became too expensive, criminals were used to feed the lethal menagerie. All the while, Caligula ordered the awnings of the amphitheatre be drawn back so contestants and spectators alike would bake in the sun.

BLOOD AND SCANDAL ON THE STREETS OF ROME

Caligula was rumoured to have had an incestuous affair with his sister Drusilla. When she died in AD 38, he ordered her to be deified and her statue placed in the Temple of Venus. While he was in mourning, it was a capital offence to laugh or even bathe. Caligula prostituted his other sisters to high-ranking Romans to win their favour. As the emperor's mental state disintegrated, even rank and status proved no defence against his whims. Nobles were branded and disfigured with hot irons and condemned to work in the mines. Some were shut up in cages on all fours, like animals, before being sawn asunder. Parents were forced to attend the executions of their own children. A senator who was a vocal critic of Caligula's rule was ordered to be torn apart alive by his fellow senators. His limbs and bowels were dragged through the streets and piled in front of the emperor. In a few short years, Caligula had alienated Rome's traditional ruling class, and his assassination in AD 41 came as no surprise. Ironically, he was stabbed to death while addressing a troupe of entertainers who had performed in his own festivities.

BOUDICA'S BLOODY VENGEANCE

In AD 43, Emperor Claudius ordered four legions to cross into Britain from Gaul. Julius Caesar had invaded in 55 and 54 BC, but only to install a friendly king. This time, the Romans were in Britain to stay, and slowly extended their rule across the island. In AD 60, the governor of Britain, Gaius Suetonius Paulinus, was campaigning in Wales. Druids opposed to Rome had concentrated on Anglesey and Paulinus led his men to face them. The disciplined Romans massacred the druids and destroyed the sacred groves where, according to Tacitus, they had performed blood sacrifices.

Meanwhile, rebellion had stirred in the east of Britain. The king of the Iceni (in what is now East Anglia) had died, leaving his lands to Rome. He hoped this would protect his widow, Boudica, and their two daughters. Instead, Rome annexed the kingdom. Boudica was flogged and her children raped. In retaliation, she raised an army of 120,000 Britons. As the main Roman army was in Wales, she was able to defeat the small forces sent against her. In quick succession she sacked Colchester and St Albans and then burned London to the ground. Seventy thousand Romans and their allies were killed in this time. Women were captured alive and had their breasts cut off and sewn to their mouths, and were then impaled lengthways.

Paulinus eventually managed to defeat the rebels in the Battle of Watling Street. After the defeat, Boudica committed suicide by taking poison. Rome was now firmly in control of Britain, and able to extend its rule into Wales and up to the Scottish border.

NERO AND THE GREAT FIRE OF ROME

Claudius Caesar Nero

Nero was the last descendant of Julius Caesar to rule Rome. He became emperor in AD 54, at the age of seventeen, and reigned until AD 68. Few rulers of Rome were as infamous or callous.

DEPRAVITY AND OPULENCE

At the start of his reign, Nero's mother Agrippina was the true ruler of Rome. Nero quickly began to wrest power from her, ordering the poisoning of his stepbrother Britannicus when Agrippina attempted to install him as emperor. Eventually Nero arranged the murder of his mother in AD 59, leaving no one to challenge him.

Nero's sexual appetites were prodigious. He would seduce married women and young boys alike. Once he castrated a youth called Sporus, dressed him as the empress and took him in his litter as a consort. The historian Suetonius claimed that one of Nero's favourite pursuits was to dress in animal skins and ravage the private parts of men and women who were tied to stakes.

Having polished off his mother, Nero also saw his first wife, Octavia, executed for adultery and, in AD 65, Nero's second wife Poppea died while pregnant. Suetonius claimed Nero had kicked her after she complained about his late return home from the races.

Nero loved obscene spectacles and would hold lavish banquets costing millions of sesterces in the Circus Maximus. Obsessed with singing, he believed that holding a lead plate to his chest and purging himself with a syringe to induce vomiting would improve his voice. He would often appear on the public stage to showcase his talents.

ROME IN RUINS

Nero's most infamous public performance was on 19 July AD 64. That day a fire started in Rome, which lasted for six days and seven nights, and destroyed 10 per cent of the city. Hundreds of citizens were trampled to death in the rush to save their property from the flames. Nero is alleged to have watched his capital burn dressed in full theatrical costume, singing a poem called the 'Sack of Ilium'. Cassius Dio claims Nero ordered the fire in order to clear space for his elaborate building plans. To forestall any accusations of arson, Nero blamed the Christian population of Rome, whom he punished cruelly – throwing them to the dogs or burning them alive to serve as torches.

Tacitus claimed that the fire was a dreadful accident and that Nero was 30 miles away in Antium at the time. While this is probable, Nero's subsequent actions were unforgiveable. He imposed heavy payments of tribute from across the empire to finance the construction plans for his colossal new palace, the *Domus Aurea* ('Golden House'). The structure was overlaid with gold and adorned with gems and mother of pearl, and the vestibule was large enough to house a 120-foot statue of himself.

Eventually Nero's policies led to revolt. In AD 68, Galba, a provincial governor, announced himself emperor. Nero's supporters quickly deserted him, and he fled Rome with the Senate preparing to declare him a public enemy. Rather than commit suicide, Nero persuaded his secretary to stab him to death.

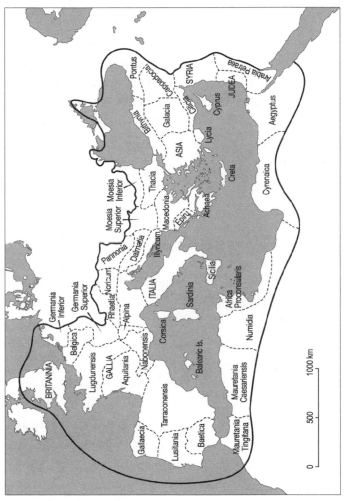

The Roman Empire at its greatest extent

THE ERUPTION OF MOUNT VESUVIUS

In AD 79, Mount Vesuvius erupted, spewing forth a cloud of stones, ash, fumes, molten rock, and pumice. After the initial explosion, pyroclastic flows destroyed the towns of Pompeii and Herculaneum and buried alive anyone who was slow in flight. A tsunami in the Bay of Naples left fish and other creatures gasping on the shore. A 'black and dreadful' cloud of ash obscured everything in sight, with the darkness only broken by the glow from fires and flashes of lightning. Sixteen thousand people died as a result of the eruption, including the naturalist Pliny the Elder, who suffocated in the fumes while trying to organize an evacuation. Three months later, Pompeii had been entirely buried in 20 feet of pumice and ash, and was not fully excavated until the eighteenth century.

DONG ZHUO

Ling of the Han Dynasty and the Emperor of China died in AD 189. Luoyang, the capital, was in turmoil as different factions at court vied for control of his son and successor Emperor Shao. Dong Zhuo, an influential warlord, marched into the city and seized control. In AD 190, Dong deposed Shao, and replaced him with his eight-year-old younger brother, Emperor Xian. Dong was now de facto head of state.

A coalition formed to remove Dong, but before they marched on Luoyang his army destroyed the capital and moved to Chang'an. Capture brought terrible punishments. Dong's preferred torture method involved binding his enemies in cloths soaked in fat and lighting a fire beneath them. Heads were left unbound so he could savour the screams. Dong hosted opulent banquets at which the entertainment was the torture of his rivals. Limbs and eyeballs were removed and tongues were cut out to prevent the victims from screaming. They were then cooked alive in boiling oil.

Dong met his end in AD 192. His foster-son Lü Bu stabbed him to death. The body was left in the streets for all to view, with a wick placed in its belly so it would burn for days. All members of Dong's clan were put to death, including his ninety-year-old mother.

CARACALLA THE KIN-SLAYER

The emperor Septimius Severus died in AD 211, leaving the Roman Empire to be ruled jointly by his children, Caracalla and Geta. The arrangement lasted less than a year. Caracalla was determined to eliminate Geta, but was foiled by his brother's bodyguards. Instead he persuaded his mother to call Geta to her apartments, ostensibly to effect a reconciliation. The ruse worked: Caracalla's men murdered Geta and he died in his mother's arms. Caracalla became sole emperor, and then embarked on a purge of Geta's friends, associates and anyone with a vague connection to him. Thousands died, their bodies piled on carts to be burned outside Rome, or thrown into ditches. Nothing stood in the way of Caracalla's whims. He left the capital in AD 213 to go on campaign.

THE MASSACRE OF ALEXANDRIA

In AD 215, Caracalla arrived in Alexandria, responding to rumours that a satire mocking him had been performed. A deputation of citizens, fearing Caracalla's reputation, lavishly hosted him. Caracalla initially played along, and then demanded all the youths of the city line up so he could assess their quality for military service. His soldiers massacred them and then plundered the city. Thousands died. Corpses were bundled into trenches to hide the extent of the slaughter.

Caracalla met a bloody end in AD 217. While on a march he stopped to urinate and was murdered by one of his bodyguards.

EMPEROR OF EXCESS

Few rulers shocked their subjects more than Elagabalus. Born in Syria, Elagabalus was the hereditary high priest of a local cult dedicated to the sun god El-Gabal. In a time of upheaval in Rome, his grandmother, who was related to the former emperor Septimius Severus, managed to gain the backing of the Roman army for Elagabalus, who rose to the imperial throne at the tender age of fourteen in AD 218. A not-so-tender Elagabalus arrived in Rome next year.

Having nothing but disdain for traditional mores, he refused to dress in Roman clothes, preferring eastern garb. He wore thick make-up and would paint his eyes. The historian Edward Gibbon states that Elagabalus 'abandoned himself to the grossest pleasures with ungoverned fury'. He was married five times, most scandalously to a vestal virgin whom he had taken by force from the temple (the order were sworn to celibacy and traditionally punished for breaking that vow by being buried alive). Elagabalus also took male lovers, whom he raised to high positions in government. There were rumours that he prostituted himself and had promised to reward any physician who would give him female genitalia. In his most brazen moment, Elagabalus made El-Gabal the chief deity of the Roman pantheon of gods, and built a lavish temple dedicated to him.

By AD 222, Elagabalus had exhausted the patience of Rome. The influential Praetorian Guard, the elite bodyguards of the emperor, switched their support to his cousin Alexander, whom they crowned emperor. Elagabalus and his mother were seized and killed. Their bodies were stripped and dragged through Rome, before being dumped in a public sewer.

THE DEATH OF ST LAWRENCE OF ROME

In AD 258, Emperor Valerian sent out an edict that all clerics were to be put to death unless they made sacrifices to Roman gods. Many Christians were martyred, and the pope himself, St Sixtus II, was beheaded on 6 August. St Lawrence had been ordered to hand over the Church's riches to the Prefect of Rome. He refused, and moved to redistribute its most valuable property to keep it from the Empire's clutches. The treasures included the alleged Holy Chalice that Jesus had used during the Last Supper, which Lawrence was able to spirit away to Spain. Lawrence was seized on 10 August and roasted alive on a red-hot gridiron. His last words were, '*Assam est; versa, et manduca!*' ('It is well done; turn it over and eat it!').

THE MASSACRE OF THESSALONICA

Theodosius I 'the Great' was emperor from AD 379 to 395. He was the last Roman ruler of both eastern and western halves of the empire and made Christianity the state religion. After his death, the two halves were never reunited, with the eastern half later becoming known as the Byzantine Empire.

Theodosius perpetrated one of the worst atrocities ordered by an emperor, when he ordered vengeance on Thessalonica in AD 390. The city was the largest in northern Greece, and had been protected – thanks to its fortifications – from the depredations of the ongoing war with the Goths, a group of Germanic tribes that were a constant threat to the empire. However, an attractive young slave-boy belonging to Butheric, the garrison commander and a Goth in the service of Rome, provided the catalyst for the disaster. The boy had caught the eye of a famed local charioteer, who attempted to rape him and was then arrested. At the next chariot race, the charioteer's absence was immediately noted and his fans were furious. The people of Thessalonica ran riot, murdering Butheric and many of his officers and dragging their corpses through the streets.

When he heard news of the murders, Theodosius ordered immediate vengeance on the city. Reconsidering his first impulse, the emperor tried to rescind the order, but it was too late. The soldiers tricked the populace of Thessalonica into crowding into the chariot arena for a supposed day of games in Theodosius's honour. As soon as the crowds were in place, the soldiers fell on them. The slaughter lasted three hours. Between 7,000 and 15,000 people were killed.

HYPATIA OF ALEXANDRIA

In the fifth century, Alexandria was a thriving city of the Roman Empire, and a major seat of learning. Hypatia, head of the Platonist School in the city and possibly the first major female mathematician, was a controversial local figure. Many believed her teachings led to unrest. Owing to her pagan beliefs, some of the city's Christians were suspicious of her and spread rumours that she practised witchcraft.

Hypatia was a vocal supporter of Orestes, the Roman prefect who disagreed with the expulsion and persecution of the city's Jewish population at the hand of the Christian Patriarch of Alexandria, Cyril. Violence flared up in AD 415, when a group of monks attacked Orestes with stones, wounding him. One of the monks was seized and tortured to death in public. Cyril's supporters sought a target against whom to retaliate. Their chosen victim was Hypatia and a crowd of Christian zealots dragged her from her chariot as she rode through the city. She was taken to a nearby church, stripped naked, and battered to death with clay tiles, which were also used to scrape off her skin. Hypatia's corpse was torn limb from limb, and carried to different churches in the city, where its fragments were burned. The assassination forced Orestes to leave Alexandria in Cyril's control.

ATTILA THE HUN'S FINAL YEAR

The Huns arrived in Europe from the steppes of Central Asia in the late fourth century. They were the scourge of Europe, their mounted archery and javelin throwers cutting a swath through those who opposed them. Their greatest leader, Attila, who reigned from AD 434, carved out a great empire that stretched far west to the Rhine. He even managed to force the once-mighty Roman Empire to pay him tribute. The negotiations must have been tense, as it was Attila's custom to execute deceitful ambassadors by nailing them to crosses and leaving their bodies to be eaten by vultures. In AD 452, Attila led his hordes into Italy, perhaps hoping to strike at Rome itself, which had been sacked by the Visigoths, a group of Germanic tribes, in AD 410.

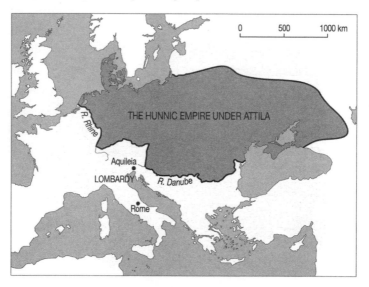

The Hunnic Empire under Attila

THE FINAL CAMPAIGN

The city of Aquileia at the head of the Adriatic, which at the time was an important political and religious centre, held out against Attila's army. Inexperienced at besieging cities, the Huns tried for three months to penetrate the fortifications, but to no avail. Deciding to give up, Attila prepared to lead his army away, until he saw a stork fly from a turret. Taking this as an omen, he launched a savage assault, which quickly caused a breach in the walls. The Huns attacked with such aggression that the ruined city was unrecognizable. Neighbouring cities were also reduced to heaps of stone and ashes, and the once fertile plains of Lombardy were ravaged. Eventually Pope Leo I managed to negotiate a truce with Attila, who then withdrew from Italy before reaching Rome.

Attila, King of the Huns

KILLED BY A NOSEBLEED?

In AD 453, Attila retired to his palace across the Danube. He had been sent a young Germanic princess called Ildico by a distant vassal hoping to curry his favour. After the raucous wedding feast and 'excessive merrymaking', Attila and his new bride retired to his tent. He had drunk a great deal of wine and, lying down on his back, suffered a major haemorrhage. This triggered a severe nosebleed and, the blood, instead of draining out, flowed down his throat, suffocating him. Attila's corpse was found the next morning, with his new wife weeping beside him. His remains were placed in a triple coffin of gold, silver, and iron. The slaves who dug his grave were executed after his burial to keep its location secret. A bawdy feast followed the funeral, but the great days for the Huns were over – Attila's children argued over their inheritance and were quickly defeated, breaking up the Hunnic Empire.

THE PLAGUE OF JUSTINIAN

In AD 541, Emperor Justinian was on the verge of conquering Italy and reuniting the eastern and western halves of the Roman Empire for the first time in over a century. Meanwhile, however, a deadly outbreak of bubonic plague, originating in Central Africa, arrived in the Byzantine Empire in Egypt. It spread quickly to North Africa and the Near East via shipping routes and, most damagingly to Justinian, it reached Constantinople (now Istanbul).

The outbreak quickly took hold in the densely packed city. Symptoms began with a sudden fever then, a few days later, bubonic swellings developed in the groin, armpits, and thighs. Some fell into deep comas; others into near-comatose states, refusing to eat or drink. Acute delirium and hallucinations followed. Eventually the swellings became gangrenous, killing the sufferer. Ten thousand people died a day.

Bodies were left unburied or thrown into tombs at random. Once the tombs were filled, corpses were packed into the city towers, and the stench of rotting flesh wafted over the city. Other bodies were loaded onto skiffs and left to drift to sea. The infrastructure of Constantinople collapsed entirely. Grain prices rose, causing starvation. At least 100,000 out of Constantinople's population of 500,000 died.

Justinian's plans to conquer Italy were foiled. Even he contracted the illness, though he survived. The plague eventually died out in AD 542 but remained endemic in the Byzantine Empire until the eighth century. It had killed a total of around 30 million people.

THE GREAT EARTHQUAKE OF ANTIOCH

In AD 526, a massive earthquake devastated Antioch, an important city in the Byzantine Empire. Antioch became, in the words of a contemporary chronicler, 'the wine press of wrath'. The initial shock was violent, but a subsequent fire caused more damage. After the blaze barely a building remained standing. Even the great church built by Constantine the Great caught fire a week after the quake and was razed to its foundations. As the wreckage was cleared, the body of the Patriarch of Antioch was found in a cauldron of pitch – he had fallen into it during the tremor and been cooked alive. The flesh had been stripped from his bones but his head remained intact.

PHOCAS, THE USURPER EMPEROR

Phocas rose from obscurity to become Byzantine emperor in AD 602. An officer in the army, he seized power from the emperor Maurice. Despite posing little threat to the new regime, Maurice was forced to witness the execution of his five sons in turn before he was beheaded. Their bodies were cast into the sea and their heads exposed to the elements until they putrefied.

OVERTHROW

Phocas's initial popularity waned. Byzantium faced attack from the Balkans and Persia. His persecution of Jewish and Christian heretics in the eastern provinces triggered numerous riots.

In AD 608, Heraclius, an important official in North Africa, revolted. Two years later, he and his army marched on Constantinople. Heraclius was proclaimed emperor and the imperial guard, led by Phocas's own son-in-law, deserted. Phocas was brought before Heraclius, stripped of his imperial garb and diadem, and was chained and dressed in ragged clothes. Heraclius asked him, 'Is this how you have ruled, wretch?', to which Phocas replied, 'And will you rule better?' Heraclius kicked Phocas to the floor.

Phocas's right arm was cut off; he was beheaded and then disembowelled. His hand and head were placed on spears and paraded through the city. His body was cut in half, dragged through the streets, and burned in a public square. Heraclius went on to reign for thirty years.

The
Medieval Era

c. AD 500 to 1450

THE DAWN OF THE VIKING AGE

THE VIKINGS WERE explorers, warriors, and traders who originated in Scandinavia. In the eighth century, they began to expand across Europe, and eventually into North America and Asia.

RAIDERS FROM THE NORTH

The first noted Viking incursion on England was their AD 793 raid of Lindisfarne Monastery on Holy Island, which is off the coast of Northumberland. The Anglo-Saxon Chronicle records that their coming was foretold by lightning and 'fiery dragons flying through the firmament'. The shallow draughts of their longships meant the

Vikings could beach directly on the shore and quickly overwhelm the monks and their monastery, causing 'lamentable havoc in the church of God'. The monks were slaughtered and their valuables ransacked. Viking raids on England continued for over two centuries. In the early eleventh century, King Cnut the Great ruled over Denmark and Norway as well as England.

THE BLOOD EAGLE

The Vikings were also adept at establishing permanent lordship over an area and laws governing new subjects were harsh. The routine punishment for robbery or murder was to be thrown from a cliff, but the most brutal retribution was the 'Blood Eagle', reserved for defeated local chieftains or kings, or any new subjects that dared kill a Viking. In this form of torture, the victim's back was hacked open with an axe and the ribs were cracked and separated from the spine. The lungs were drawn out of the open wound, sprinkled with salt, and then draped over the victim's back to resemble bloody wings. Fortunately, the victim usually died very soon after – either from suffocation, shock, or loss of blood.

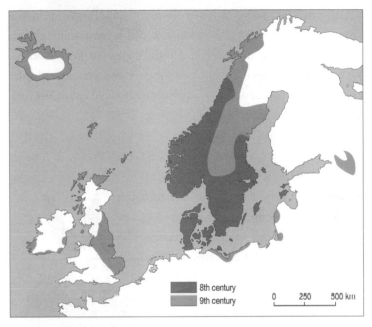

Viking conquests in the eighth and ninth centuries

8th century
9th century

0   250   500 km

THE LAST ANGLO-SAXON
KING OF ENGLAND

Harold Godwinson became king in January 1066. His predecessor was his brother-in-law, the childless Edward the Confessor. Edward had allegedly promised the throne to Duke William of Normandy. The Normans, who were descended from Norse Vikings, were an influential presence in England. Edward's mother was a Norman (William's great-aunt), he had spent many years in Normandy before he became king, and he had many Norman advisors and supporters. Therefore, it seemed natural for Edward to name William as his successor, but on his deathbed he changed his mind.

William began making plans to invade England to press his claim to the throne. Harold also faced a counter-claim from the King of Norway. The Norwegians invaded Yorkshire in September, but Harold defeated them at Stamford Bridge, the battle turning in Harold's favour with the death of a Norwegian warrior, who had been holding a bridge single-handedly. But Harold had no time to savour his victory – William's army had crossed the Channel, so he was forced to march his exhausted army south.

The two forces drew up against each other near Hastings on 14 October. Harold had the high ground, and his army managed to hold out against Norman attacks. It appeared the day would end in

The wounding of Harold at the Battle of Hastings

stalemate until William ordered his army to pretend to retreat, and some of the English troops rushed to follow them, throwing their lines into disorder. The Normans then advanced. William ordered his archers to shoot upwards so the arrows would rain down on the English from above. Many historians believe it was one of these arrows that killed Harold, piercing him in the eye. Others believe he was ridden down by Norman knights and hacked to pieces with swords. Whatever the cause, William marched on to London and claimed the throne. All subsequent monarchs of England have been his descendants.

THE GRANADA MASSACRE

In 1066, Granada in Spain was the capital of a Muslim emirate, under King Badis. However, the real power behind the throne was his Jewish vizier Joseph ibn-Nagrella, a fact that made Joseph unpopular with the local Berbers. A rumour emerged that Joseph was planning to kill Badis and seize power himself. On 30 December, a mob stormed the palace, captured Joseph and crucified him. The violence spread to the Jewish population, who many believed had grown too influential in the kingdom. Three thousand people were killed. The massacre was a watershed in Moorish Spain – marking a change from general tolerance of Jews to intermittent anti-Semitic violence. In 1492, the Catholic monarchs, Ferdinand and Isabella, expelled all Jews from Spain.

THE TOWER OF LONDON

In the aftermath of the Norman invasion of England, William the Conqueror moved to impose his authority. The most long-standing symbol of this was the Tower of London.

PLACE OF EXECUTION:
THE PEASANTS' REVOLT

In 1381, the common men of England rose up in the greatest popular revolt in the country's history. There was unrest across England, but it was most concentrated and aggressive in the south-east. The peasants' figurehead, Wat Tyler, marched on London and delivered his demands to the young king, Richard II. Meanwhile, another band of peasants stormed the Tower; the royal chambers were invaded and looted. The unpopular Lord Chancellor Simon Sudbury (also the Archbishop of Canterbury) was hauled out of the chapel by the mob and his head was forced on to a block. The executioner was no professional – it took eight strokes to hack through his neck. Sudbury's mitre was then nailed to his head, which was paraded round the city. The revolt subsided with the death of Tyler, who was killed by the Lord Mayor of London during a meeting with the king.

THE PRINCES IN THE TOWER

In April 1483, the twelve-year-old Edward V succeeded his father Edward IV. His uncle Richard of Gloucester installed himself as

The Bloody Tower

protector, and confined Edward and his younger brother to the Tower. In June, Richard assumed the kingship while the princes remained imprisoned. Supporters plotted to rescue them, forcing Richard's hand; he allegedly ordered that they be murdered to prevent an uprising. The princes' exact fate and the circumstances around their deaths are unknown, although the skeletons of two children were found in the Tower during renovations in 1674.

THE PEOPLE'S CRUSADE: FROM COLOGNE TO CANNIBALISM

In November 1095, Pope Urban II preached a Crusade to aide Byzantium against Turkish attack and reconquer Jerusalem. The message set Europe aflame. Rather than attracting only knights and nobles, peasants and townsfolk also responded with great fervour. A monk called Peter the Hermit journeyed across Europe gathering public support. By April 1096, he had amassed a motley army of 40,000, almost exclusively untrained and ill-equipped, and including numerous women and children. They set out for Jerusalem from Cologne.

Peter the Hermit

The first sign of trouble came at Niš, where a quarrel with locals led to the town's garrison attacking the Crusaders. By the time they reached Constantinople in August, their number had shrunk to 30,000. As they continued their march across Asia Minor, disputes saw factions forming. By 21 October, only 20,000 remained to march out of Nicaea. A Turkish army ambushed them outside of

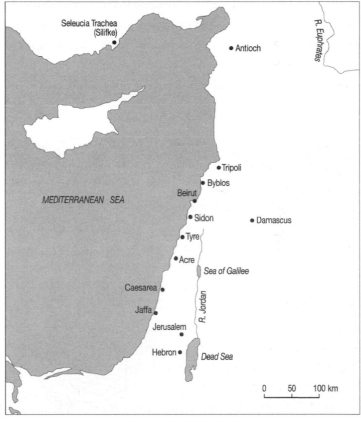

Sites in the Holy Land

the city. By noon most of the Crusaders had been massacred, except for a handful of attractive boys and girls who were enslaved. A small number of the People's Crusade survived to form a ragged corps called the Tafurs. Barefoot, filthy, clad in sackcloth, and armed with clubs and sticks, they lived on roots and grass, and sometimes the roasted corpses of their enemies.

In spite of the failure of Peter the Hermit's expedition, the First Crusade was otherwise a great success. The Princes' Crusade, which arrived in the Holy Land in 1097 and was more organized, absorbed the remnants of the People's Crusade. Jerusalem was captured in 1099, and a Christian kingdom was established there.

HOW AN ATTACK OF INDIGESTION LED TO NINETEEN YEARS OF CIVIL WAR

Henry I was the son of William the Conqueror, and had ruled England since 1100. In 1135, during a visit to Normandy to see his daughter Matilda, Henry died. The cause was indigestion following an overindulgence of lampreys. The boneless eel-like creature was a particular favourite of Henry's, and celebrated for its soft and oily flesh. Henry had made Matilda his heir, but she faced a challenge from her cousin Stephen of Blois. Their battle for the English throne was known as 'the Anarchy', and only settled in 1154 when Stephen agreed to make Matilda's son Henry his heir. When Stephen died suddenly that October, Henry peacefully inherited the kingdom.

A KING KILLED BY BEDCLOTHES

Alaungsithu had ruled Burma since 1113. Aged eighty-one and king for over half a century, Alaungsithu fell ill and slipped into unconsciousness. Narathu, his son, saw a chance to seize power and moved his father from the palace to a temple. Alaungsithu eventually came round, and was furious. Narathu hastened to the temple, determined to become king. He seized his father's bedclothes and, forcing them over his face, smothered him to death. In Narathu's quest for power he also poisoned his brother. But the new king's malevolent ways came back to bite him – he was killed in 1170 by agents of a chief whose daughter he had murdered.

MURDER IN THE CATHEDRAL: THE DEATH OF THOMAS BECKET

Thomas Becket had been Henry II's Lord Chancellor, one of the most important offices in the kingdom. Henry made him Archbishop of Canterbury in 1162, believing that Becket would favour the crown over the interests of the Catholic Church. Henry was mistaken: Becket became a vigorous defender of the Church's rights, and he and Henry became estranged.

The spark for violence came in June 1170. The Archbishop of York crowned Henry's son junior king (to ensure an unopposed succession – although Henry the Young King died in 1183, before his father), impinging on the Archbishop of Canterbury's right to crown English monarchs. In December, Becket excommunicated all the prelates who had been involved in the coronation.

The murder of Thomas Becket

Henry, holding court in Normandy, was enraged: 'What miserable … traitors have I … promoted … who let their lord be treated with such shameful contempt by a low-born clerk!' he thundered. A delegation was sent to arrest Becket. Shadowing them were four knights stung into action by Henry's words. The knights arrived in Canterbury before the official delegation and confronted Becket at the cathedral on 29 December. Insults flew. Becket refused to surrender, believing the sanctity of the cathedral would protect him. It did not. The knights struck at Becket with their swords. The first blow sliced off the top of Becket's head, and he fell to the floor. The killing blow was then delivered with such force that the sword lay broken on the stone floor.

In 1171, a popular belief in the curative power of Becket's blood began, and he was canonized in 1173. Henry's political nous enabled him to survive the scandal caused by Becket's assassination, and the threat of being excommunicated from the Church, which would have been disastrous for the king of a Catholic country. He negotiated a settlement with the Pope, agreeing to go on Crusade (although he never did). As part of the settlement, Henry was forced to make public repentance for the murder in 1174. Approaching Canterbury wearing a hair shirt, he walked the last mile to the cathedral. At Becket's tomb he prostrated himself and was publicly whipped. Henry spent the night fasting and praying near the tomb.

ANDRONIKUS KOMNENOS

By the twelfth century, the once great Byzantine Empire had diminished significantly. Emperor Manuel I Komnenos struggled to hold the realm together. He faced near-constant strife from his cousin, the irrepressible rogue Andronikus.

PHILANDERING ACROSS
BYZANTIUM AND BEYOND

In the 1150s, Andronikus was a favourite at court, despite the fact he had taken the emperor's niece as his mistress. In 1153, Andronikus began conspiring against Manuel, and was imprisoned. He escaped in 1165 and somehow managed to win his way back into Manuel's good graces, being appointed to an imperial governorship. Andronikus was more interested in intrigue than administration. In a visit to the Crusader Kingdom of Antioch in 1166, he caused a scandal by seducing the younger sister of its ruler. The two stole away to Jerusalem. There he moved on to Theodora, the twenty-one-year-old widow of the former King of Jerusalem, and Manuel's niece. Infuriated, Manuel ordered that Andronikus be extradited to Constantinople. The couple fled east into exile.

THE MASSACRE OF THE LATINS

Manuel died in 1180, leaving his ten-year-old son Alexios II as his successor. Manuel had been unpopular among his Greek subjects for favouring the Latins – the non-Greek residents of Constantinople –

and the Crusader kings. Alexios's mother, the Latin Maria of Antioch, was named regent, leading to popular discontent. Wicked Andronikus took advantage of the unpopularity of Maria's rule by marching on Constantinople in 1182 and seizing power, making himself co-emperor with Alexios. The Greek population of the city rose up against the Latins, rampaging through their quarter. No one was spared. The papal legate was decapitated, and his head tied to the tail of a dog to be dragged through the streets. Tens of thousands were massacred or fled, and 4,000 were sold into slavery to the Turks. Andronikus then forced Alexios to sign the execution warrant for his own mother, who was killed by strangulation. The next year Andronikus had Alexios put to death and became the sole emperor.

THE DEATH OF EMPEROR ANDRONIKUS

Andronikus's rule quickly grew unpopular. He became increasingly paranoid, blinding or hanging men at the slightest suspicion. When the Norman dukes of Sicily invaded Byzantine lands, panic-stricken Andronikus ordered mass arrests and executions. In September 1185, an official called Isaac Angelos managed to win the favour of the people of Constantinople and seized power. Andronikus was captured, paraded around the city on a mangy camel and then handed over to the mob. For three days he was tied to a post to be subject to their depredations: his teeth and hair were pulled out; boiling water was poured on his face; one of his hands was hacked off; and his eye was gouged out. He was finally hung by his feet and stabbed to death. Isaac proved to be an ineffectual emperor, and his rule hastened Byzantium's steady decline.

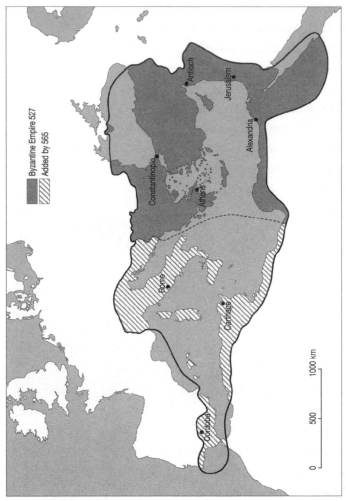

The Byzantine Empire at its greatest extent

THE FALL OF ACRE

In the late twelfth century, the Kurdish Muslim Saladin had recaptured Jerusalem and much of the Holy Land. The Third Crusade was an attempt to reverse this.

The most brutal episode of the conflict was at Acre, a vital port city held by the Muslims, which the Crusaders besieged in October 1189. In June 1191, King Richard I of England ('Richard the Lionheart') and King Philip II Augustus of France had arrived with sizeable armies. After a bloody struggle, on 12 July Acre surrendered. The Crusaders marched in and imprisoned the garrison. King Richard was in command of negotiations for their return. The garrison was to be exchanged for money, captured Crusaders, and a piece of the True Cross.

On 11 August, Saladin sent over the first of three instalments of money and prisoners. Richard insisted it was insufficient and refused to release any captives. In turn, Saladin broke off negotiations. After nine days Richard, eager to move on to Jerusalem, brought the situation to a head. He declared that Saladin had broken the bargain, and ordered the garrison be put to death. Richard's forces joyfully slaughtered the 2,700 defenceless men, thanking God for the chance to avenge their fallen comrades. Only a handful of notables and those strong enough to be sold into slave labour were spared.

On 22 August, Richard led his men out of Acre. Saladin was able to cut off a group of stragglers equal in size to Acre's slaughtered garrison. His army killed them all, sparing only the washerwomen.

THE MASSACRE OF BÉZIERS

The Cathars, a medieval Christian dualist sect, became widespread in the Languedoc region of southern France during the eleventh and twelfth centuries. In an attempt to wipe them out, the Pope declared a Crusade in 1209. On 21 July, a Crusader army marched on Béziers and ordered the town to hand over any Cathars. The townspeople refused, and a lengthy siege appeared imminent.

The next day, however, a rag-tag group of Crusader followers known as the *ribauds* stormed the gates of Béziers armed with picks and clubs. As they breached the town's defences, armoured Crusader knights rushed to join battle. At this point the papal legate, Arnaud Amalric, is alleged to have given his fateful counsel to the Crusaders: 'Kill them all, God will know His own.'

What followed was a brutal massacre. Fewer than one in ten of the people of Béziers were Cathars, yet the Crusaders spared no one. Some townspeople sought sanctuary in the cathedral, but to no end. The chronicler William of Tudela recorded: 'No cross or altar or crucifix could save them ... they killed the clergy too, and

the women and the children. I doubt if one person came out alive.'
Once the looting was over, the Crusaders set the town alight. In the
space of a few hours Béziers was transformed into a lifeless pile of
rubble. 'The workings of divine vengeance have been wondrous,'
Arnaud triumphantly informed the Pope.

THE KING WHO DIED PLAYING POLO

Qutb-ud-din Aibak was sold into slavery as a child. Eventually he
came into the ownership of Shahabuddin Muhammad Ghauri, who
had carved out a sultanate that ruled over Afghanistan, Pakistan, and
northern India. Aibak became Shahabuddin's most trusted man.
When his master died in 1206, Aibak established himself as his
successor (after receiving his official manumission), ruling as sultan
from his capital in Delhi. Aibak was a popular ruler, known for his
gallantry, but his reign was brief. He died in 1210 playing polo in
Lahore. He tumbled and his horse fell on him; the saddle pommel
pierced his breast, causing a fatal wound.

THE CHILDREN'S CRUSADE

In 1212, a twelve-year-old shepherd boy called Stephen appeared
at the court of King Philip II of France. Stephen told the king
Christ had appeared to him in a vision, instructing him to preach a
Crusade to Jerusalem to convert the Muslims. Philip, unimpressed,
told the boy to return home. Stephen was undeterred, and preached
his message regardless. He travelled across France and by June
had amassed a large following of several thousand children and

young people. They marched to Marseilles, where Stephen had told them the Mediterranean would part for them as the Red Sea had done for Moses. Disheartened when this did not happen, many returned home. Two local merchants, Hugh the Iron and William the Pig, offered Stephen and his followers free passage to the Holy Land. They set off in seven ships, but never arrived at their destination. For eighteen years their fate remained a mystery.

In 1230, a traveller from the east arrived in France. He claimed to have been one of the children who left Marseilles in 1212. Two of the ships had been wrecked off Sardinia, and sunk with all hands. The rest were captured by Saracens and the children taken to Algeria to be sold as slaves. Some were shipped on to Egypt and others further afield to the slave market in Baghdad, where many were martyred for not accepting Islam. Stephen and his followers had been tricked by the two French merchants who were in league with the slavers.

GENGHIS KHAN AND THE RISE OF THE MONGOLS

In 1206, Genghis established himself as the khan, or emperor, of the nomadic tribes of Central Asia. Sweeping down from the steppes in massed ranks of horsemen, the Mongol hordes were the most formidable army in the world. The Mongol Empire would eventually stretch from China to Russia and into Central Asia and the Middle East – one of the largest empires the world had ever seen.

WAR WITH CHINA

In 1211, the ambassador from the Chinese Jin Dynasty arrived at Genghis's court, and demanded Genghis kowtow to the emperor. Genghis refused and began preparing for war. Two years later the Mongols advanced to the Jin capital, Zhongdu (Beijing). After besieging the capital they withdrew, having been given a large tribute. In 1214, the Mongol army again approached Zhongdu, and attacked its formidable defences. The Chinese relief army was defeated and hope deserted the terrified people of the city, who began to resort to cannibalism. The commanding Jin general committed suicide when it was clear the city was lost.

Zhongdu surrendered in May 1215. The city was violently sacked and looted – and burned for a month. Half a century later, Genghis's grandson Kublai Khan would rule over China, establishing the Mongol Yuan Dynasty.

MASTER OF TERROR

Genghis was expert at instilling fear in his enemies. When he and his army captured a city, each Mongol warrior was ordered to kill a certain number of people. As proof the orders had been carried out, the warriors were required to collect the ears of the slain in sacks for their commanding officers to count. A few days after each massacre, troops returned to the city to search for anyone hiding in the ruins – and kill them. These tactics spread terror, and ensured that many cities would surrender to the Mongols rather than face their army, in the hope they would be merciful.

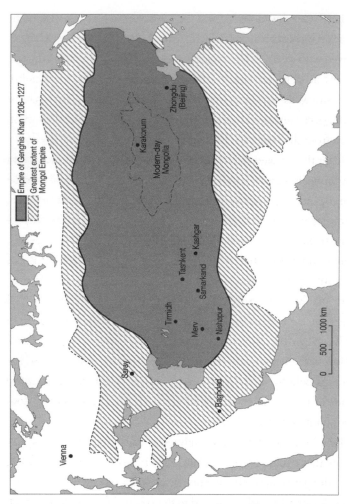

The Mongol Empire under Genghis Khan

Empire of Genghis Khan 1206–1227

Greatest extent of Mongol Empire

Zhongdu (Beijing)

Karakorum

Modern-day Mongolia

Kashgar

Tashkent

Samarkand

Termidh

Merv

Nishapur

Saray

Baghdad

Vienna

0   500   1000 km

THE MONGOLS MOVE WEST

In 1219, Genghis moved against the Khwarezmid Empire in Iran. The area was highly urbanized, which the nomadic tent-dwelling Mongols viewed with disdain. The invaders were therefore particularly brutal. Expert at siege warfare, the Mongols used saltpetre to demolish defensive walls. Prisoners were wantonly employed to fill in moats or to drag siege engines towards fortifications as arrows rained down on them from the besieged cities. The Mongols showed little mercy.

After they sacked Tirmidh (in modern Uzbekistan) a captive told the Mongols she had swallowed a pearl, in the hope she would be spared. Instead, a warrior ripped her open and extracted the pearl from her intestines. Genghis then gave orders that all the corpses were to be disembowelled in case others had swallowed pearls. When Merv (located in modern Turkmenistan) fell in 1221, 700,000 inhabitants were butchered, and only eighty craftsmen were spared. The Iranian city of Nishapur was the target of special attention, as Genghis's son-in-law Tokuchar had been killed there in 1220. When the Mongols returned the following year, Tokuchar's widow was charged with overseeing the slaughter. Everyone in the city was beheaded, and separate pyramids were formed from the heads of men, women and children. Even the city's cats and dogs were hunted down and killed.

By 1241, the Mongols had advanced as far west as Austria, but before they could press on further Genghis's son, Khan Ögedei, died. The Mongol armies returned home to elect a successor. The power struggles after Ögedei's death led to the eventual fragmentation of the empire, and his successors were more interested in consolidating their power in Asia and Russia than invading Western Europe.

THE SACK OF BAGHDAD

Baghdad was the capital of the Abbasid Caliphate, which had stretched all the way to Spain from the eighth to the mid-ninth centuries. The city was the greatest of the Islamic world, and the centre of art and learning. In 1257, a Mongol army of 150,000 led by Hulegu Khan descended on Baghdad. Hulegu offered the Caliph Al-Musta'sim the chance to surrender and hand over the city, but he refused. The people of Baghdad would come to regret this. The caliph sent out an army but they were either drowned or cut down by horsemen as Hulegu smashed the nearby dams, flooding the battlefield. Survivors fled back to Baghdad and the Mongols besieged the city, bombarding its walls with Chinese explosives.

On 10 February 1258, Baghdad surrendered. Hulegu took the caliph and his family captive, and executed all remaining soldiers. The Mongol army humbled the once-great city. The palace, grand mosque, and tombs of the caliphs were burned down and the famed libraries were ransacked – the waters of the Tigris reportedly turned black with the ink from the books and manuscripts. On one street forty newborns were found without mothers; they were slaughtered immediately. At least 100,000 people were massacred.

All the while, Al-Musta'sim had been forced to watch the carnage. After ten days he was put out of his misery: the Mongols rolled him up in a carpet to be trampled by horses. Hulegu went on to conquer the rest of the region, establishing the Ilkhanate, which ruled over much of Central Asia and the Middle East.

THE DEADLY ASSASSINS

The Assassins were a fanatical Muslim sect established in the late-eleventh century. Their founder was Hassan-i-Sabbah, who sought to create a disciplined order of warriors to further his own political ends by eliminating his enemies, both Muslim and Christian. The Assassins' headquarters were a formidable mountain citadel called the Eagle's Nest at Alamut in Persia. Expert in covert infiltration and disguise, the sect came close to killing Saladin, the great Muslim leader, on two occasions. In 1192, they killed Conrad of Montferrat, the king-elect of Jerusalem, as he walked home one evening. This act was a great blow to the Crusader cause.

UNDERCOVER ASSASSINATION

The Assassins diminished in number in the thirteenth century, but were robust enough to commit one last murder. In 1270, Philip of Montfort, Lord of Tyre, was the strongest Crusader lord left in the Holy Lands, which were being progressively conquered by the Muslim Mamluks. Fearing his ability to win allies in Europe, the Assassins were called on to eliminate him. One of their fanatics was sent to Tyre. Pretending to be a Christian convert, he inveigled himself into Philip's presence. While Philip was at prayer, the Assassin stabbed him, inflicting a mortal wound. Philip died in his son's arms. The next year the Ninth Crusade was launched, but it had little impact. By the end of the thirteenth century, the Crusader presence in the Holy Land had virtually vanished.

STRIFE IN THE KINGDOM
OF DENMARK

An important political theme in medieval Europe was the struggle of the various monarchies to impose their will over the Church and the nobility. In Denmark this led to the assassination of two kings in succession: Christopher I and his son Eric V.

AT WAR WITH THE CHURCH

On ascending the throne in 1252, Christopher I attempted to force the Church to pay the same property taxes as any other landholder. This led to a dispute with Jacob Erlandsen, the wealthy and powerful Archbishop of Lund, who then excommunicated the king. In response, Christopher hauled the archbishop before him and stripped him of his clerical garb, forcing him to wear secular clothing and a fool's cap. The archbishop was then paraded in public and put into prison. In 1259, the king died suddenly. An abbot murdered him by slipping poison into his communion wine.

AT WAR WITH THE NOBLES

Christopher's son Eric proved to be a poor king. He rarely kept a promise and was nicknamed 'Klipping' for devaluing the currency by clipping coins (decreasing the gold and silver in a coin by shaving the precious metal off its circumference but continuing to circulate it at face value). Although Eric made peace with the Church, he offended the nobility, causing a cabal of influential men to plot his murder. They struck in 1286. After a day's hunting in Jutland, Eric and his party retired to a barn for the night. A group of assassins, dressed as Franciscan monks, set upon the king and stabbed him to death. When his corpse was found in the morning, it was reported to have suffered fifty-six knife wounds.

THE EXECUTION OF
WILLIAM WALLACE

In the 1290s, English monarch Edward I had won control of Scotland – then an independent kingdom – but faced resistance. In May 1297, William Wallace emerged from obscurity to become a rebel leader when he killed an English sheriff. He became a major figure in the rebellion and had many victories before his defeat at Falkirk in 1298. Wallace returned to Scotland from exile in 1303 but was seized in August 1305 and brought to London to stand trial, having been charged with murder, arson, destruction of property and sacrilege.

Wallace was marched into Westminster Hall where, with a laurel wreath placed mockingly on his brow, he was found guilty and sentenced to be hanged, drawn, and quartered. The route taken to Smithfield, his place of execution, was circuitous, and over the 4 miles he faced the scorn of the people of London. At Smithfield Wallace was hanged until close to death before being cut down to have his heart and bowels gouged out and burned before him. He was then beheaded and his corpse was cut into quarters. His head was placed on London Bridge but the four quarters of his body were sent to Newcastle (to be exhibited above a common sewer), Berwick, Stirling, and Perth.

It appeared Edward I had won over Scotland. But in 1306, Wallace's compatriot Robert the Bruce was crowned King of Scotland and, following Edward I's death in 1307, Edward II proved a poor leader. In 1314, Robert defeated the English at Bannockburn, winning Scottish independence. Scotland remained a separate kingdom until the early eighteenth century, and Wallace was remembered as a great patriot.

THE MURDER OF EDWARD II

Edward II became king in 1307. Civil unrest characterized his reign, compounded by his excessively generous gifts to male favourites rumoured to be his lovers. The first of these favourites was Piers Gaveston, who grew so unpopular among England's nobles that he was forced into exile on three occasions. When he returned for the final time in 1312, he was treated as an outlaw and hunted down and beheaded. Edward's wife, Isabella, manoeuvred to remove her husband and place their son on the throne. In 1326, Edward's latest favourite, Hugh Despenser, was hanged, drawn, and quartered, as well as castrated. Edward was forced to abdicate and was imprisoned at Berkeley Castle, where he was placed in a cell adjoining a pit filled with rotting flesh.

No one visited Edward. In October 1327, Isabella sent an agent to execute him. One chronicler cites strangulation as the cause of death, but others suggest Edward had a red-hot iron inserted into his anus. It is said that his screams can still be heard in Berkeley Castle.

THE END OF THE KNIGHTS TEMPLAR

The Order of the Temple (known as the Knights Templar) was founded in Jerusalem in 1119. It was formed of Christian knights and clerics who dedicated themselves to protecting the Crusader kingdoms in the Holy Land. With numerous bequests of land and money, the Templars built up huge assets and effectively became a trans-European bank.

King Philip IV of France owed a fortune to the Templar bankers. So that he could be free of his debts, he decided to undermine the Templars by capitalizing on rumours of their alleged impropriety. In September 1307, Philip sent instruction to royal officials across France to begin preparations for wholesale arrests of Templars. The axe fell on Friday 13 October. All members of the order in France were arrested and their property was sequestered. Once captured, the Templars were subjected to starvation and torture. They were forced to admit to all manner of erroneous accusations under duress, including that on admission to the order they were made to deny Christ and spit on his image. They were then brought naked before a senior official to be kissed on the spine, navel, mouth and buttocks. Many also admitted to carnal relations with other members of the Order, and to worshipping false idols.

In May 1310, fifty-four Templars who had denied all charges were burned alive outside Paris. In 1312, Philip was able to force the Pope to officially condemn the Templars, and the Order that had once held sway over princes and kings ceased to exist. In 1314, the final Grand Master of the order, Jacques de Molay, was burned at the stake outside Notre Dame Cathedral.

THE BLACK DEATH

In the 1340s, the most devastating pandemic in European history struck: the Black Death. Precise death tolls are impossible to calculate, but it is likely that by 1420 the population of the continent had shrunk by one-third. The virus is thought to have originated in China and reached Europe in 1346 through the Genoese trade colony of Kaffa in the Crimea, when a Mongol khan used siege catapults to hurl plague-ridden corpses over the city's walls. By 1348, the plague had rapidly spread across Europe and reached as far as Russia, where it claimed the life of the Grand Duke of Muscovy.

The Dance of Death

PESTILENCE IN THE CITIES

Europe's densely packed and unhygienic urban areas suffered the worst death tolls. Families abandoned sick relatives in their homes. Pest houses were hastily established for the sick and bodies were dumped en masse in plague pits. Europe's Jewish community frequently bore the brunt of the blame for the plague – in 1349 in Strasbourg, 900 of the city's Jewish population were burned alive. Pope Clement VI appealed against the anti-Semitic violence but to no avail.

Hundreds of thousands of pilgrims marched from town to town, sleeping outside and gathering in public spaces to confess their sins. Many of them were flagellants, who would also strip to the waist and whip themselves with knotted cords or leather thongs tipped with metal studs, hoping that the spilled blood would assuage God's wrath. Europe's population did not recover to pre-plague levels until the 1600s.

KING CHARLES THE MAD

Between 1392 and 1422, France faced the ongoing Hundred Years' War with England while its king, Charles VI, descended into madness.

THE FIRST OUTBREAK

In August 1392, rumours began spreading of Charles uttering 'silly' words and making obscene gestures 'unbecoming to royalty', as if he were beginning to lose his senses. While riding with his retinue, a leper unsettled Charles by accosting him and later he was alarmed by the sound of a page dropping his lance. Charles panicked, drew his sword, and attacked his brother. In the melee, the king killed five men before he could be subdued. He was taken to a castle and remained in a fugue state for two days.

DESCENT INTO MADNESS

After his initial attack, Charles was plagued by frequent periods of insanity. In 1395, he suffered a seven-month bout during which he did not recognize his wife or children. When he saw his coat of arms he tried to erase it, claiming he was not king and his name was George. He ran through his palace until he was physically exhausted and the entrances had to be barricaded to prevent his escape. In another bout in 1405, Charles refused to bathe, shave or change his clothes for five months. When he was finally persuaded to don new attire, his body was covered in filthy boils. By the time of Charles's death in 1422, France was totally beleaguered by the English and the allied Duchy of Burgundy (a powerful independent duchy in eastern France), with large swaths of territory under foreign control.

THE MARTYRDOM OF JOAN OF ARC

In 1429, the English were besieging Orléans and on the verge of overrunning France. Salvation came in the form of a seventeen-year-old peasant girl named Joan of Arc. Inspired by visions from saints and angels telling her to drive the English out of France, Joan travelled to court to seek audience with the king. Having impressed the monarch, she led the relief of Orléans and inspired the French to turn the tide of the war.

In 1430, Joan was captured by the Burgundians. She was sold to the English, who tried her for heresy. On 30 May 1431, Joan was found guilty. The court cast her out of the church, claiming she was 'infected with the leprosy of heresy'. Joan was bound to a pillar and burned alive. Her remains were burned twice more and her ashes thrown into the Seine.

THE MONSTER OF MACHECOUL

Gilles de Rais was a Breton knight and general who fought alongside Joan of Arc during the Hundred Years' War. His story is the origin of the 'Bluebeard' fable about a bloodthirsty noble who murders his wives. The truth is even more horrific.

When his uncle died in 1432, Gilles inherited a huge fortune. About a year later, he retired to Brittany where he used his inheritance to fund a lavish lifestyle. No one suspected Gilles would turn to murder and child abuse for his entertainments. With the help of accomplices, he soon began luring children to his castle in Machecoul. His first recorded victim was a twelve-year-old boy who was pampered and given rich food and drink. He was then taken to a private room and hung by the neck to stifle his screams while Gilles sexually abused and then killed him. Gilles repeated this practice with dozens of other children who were either decapitated or had their necks broken. He would continue his abuse of the corpses while they were still warm, kissing them and cutting them open to admire their innards. The bodies were burned and then thrown into moats or cesspits.

By 1436, Gilles was running out of money, so he began studying black magic and alchemy to raise funds, using body parts of his victims in his spells. In 1440, the Duke of Brittany, having heard rumours of the murders, had Gilles arrested. During the trial Gilles made a full confession and was sentenced to death. He was hanged on 26 October, leaving at least thirty-five known victims – the true number was probably higher.

The
Renaissance

c. 1450 to 1570

VLAD THE IMPALER

P RINCE VLAD III of Wallachia (in modern-day Romania) was
the historical figure behind Bram Stoker's *Dracula*. Although
he did not practise vampirism, his rule was certainly bloody.
Born in Transylvania in 1431, he was the son of Vlad the Dragon,
from whom he inherited the sobriquet Dracula, 'son of the dragon'.

When he became prince in 1456, one of Vlad's main problems
was the growing power of the boyars, who were the leading
aristocratic families of Wallachia. His solution was brutal. After
feasting the boyars and their families, several hundred were seized
and impaled in his courtyard. Any survivors were shackled and
forced to work on rebuilding one of Vlad's palaces. Impalement is
one the cruellest forms of execution. The victim is pierced with a

Vertical impalement

sharpened stake thrust up through the body. Death comes slowly – a victim could face hours, sometimes days, of agony.

Vlad reserved his greatest cruelty for the Saxons, who had settled in neighbouring territory. He frequently raided their settlements, burning entire villages and massacring the inhabitants. Some were impaled, while others were buried to the waist and shot. No one was spared. A contemporary chronicle recorded that 'he had people impaled, usually indiscriminately, young and old, women and men'. Mothers had their breasts cut off and the heads of their babies were forced into the wounds. Others were burned alive and 'hacked into pieces like a head of cabbage'. Vlad also roasted children, whose mothers 'had to eat their children themselves'.

THE END OF
THE BYZANTINE EMPIRE

By 1453, the Ottomans had completely overrun Byzantium, extending their territory from Anatolia into the Balkans. Only the formidable walls of Constantinople prevented the city's capture. Sultan Mehmed II was determined to seize Constantinople, a centre of Christian faith and imperial prestige. He had an army of 100,000, as well as a large fleet. The sultan completely surrounded Constantinople by sea and land. Constantine XI, the final Byzantine emperor, had only a garrison of 8,000 and some foreign volunteers. After some initial attacks, the Turks launched a determined assault on 29 May, breaching the city walls. Emperor Constantine was killed trying to lead a counterattack. His capital stood open to the Turkish army.

THE SACK OF CONSTANTINOPLE

Mehmed granted his men three days to loot the city. Anyone they met in the streets – man, woman, or child – was killed. Palaces, churches and holy houses were ransacked. Many monks and nuns flung themselves down well shafts to avoid capture. Reportedly, 'blood flowed like rainwater' in the city and bodies floated out to sea like 'melons along a canal'. Four thousand civilians and soldiers were killed.

Mehmed left Constantinople on 21 June. As he rode through the rubble, the sultan was moved to tears by the destruction, and vowed to rebuild the city. He was true to his word, and by the end of his reign in 1481, it had been resurrected with splendid architecture and its population had grown fourfold.

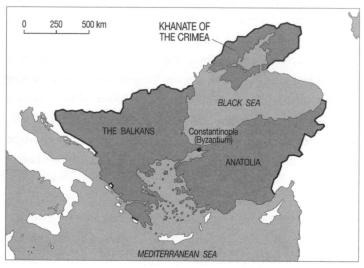

The Ottoman Empire under Mehmed II

THE RISE OF RODRIGO BORGIA

The popes of Renaissance Rome were not merely pontiffs but powerful secular rulers, governing a large swath of central Italy called the Papal States. They were no strangers to violence, feuding, and debauchery: none more so than Alexander VI, born Rodrigo Borgia.

Rodrigo was favoured by his uncle Calixtus III, the first Borgia pope. At the age of twenty-five he was made a cardinal, appointed the Bishop of Valencia, and granted the lucrative office of Vice-Chancellor. Rodrigo amassed a huge personal fortune by taking bribes and forging documents to license incestuous marriages. He was infamous for holding lavish orgies and was described by a contemporary as a man of 'endless virility'. Pope Pius II upbraided him for acting like one of 'the most vulgar young men of the age'.

In 1473, returning from a visit to Valencia, Rodrigo was shipwrecked off the coast of Tuscany. Convalescing in Pisa, he met Vannozza dei Cattanei, a famed courtesan. She would become his most longstanding mistress and bear him four children. In 1492, Rodrigo became pope, as Alexander VI, after bribing at least thirteen cardinals at the conclave (a meeting convened to elect a new pope).

POPE ALEXANDER VI
AND HIS CHILDREN

One of Alexander's first acts was to make his eighteen-year-old son Cesare a cardinal. Cesare had a sadistic streak: he was known for using criminals for target practice. He also hated his older brother Giovanni, who had been given command of the papal armies. The situation was compounded when Giovanni seduced Cesare's mistress.

In 1497, Giovanni disappeared after he and Cesare had dined at their mother's house. His body was found in the Tiber, disfigured by stab wounds. Cesare sensationally resigned as cardinal and assumed his brother's office, later carving out a small territory in northern Italy and becoming a successful mercenary general.

The Borgias continued to court scandal. There were rumours of incest between Alexander and his daughter Lucrezia, as well as between Lucrezia and her brothers. In 1500, Cesare engineered the murder of Lucrezia's husband Alfonso, the son of the King of Naples, against whom Cesare had recently allied with France. Cesare's agents attacked Alfonso and tried to stab him to death. The attempt failed, and Alfonso recovered from his wounds, only to be strangled in his bed while recuperating.

In 1501, Cesare hosted a notorious party in the Vatican known as the Banquet of Chestnuts. The floor was strewn with chestnuts and the naked guests, including Alexander and Lucrezia, as well as numerous prostitutes, crawled around picking them up before copulating.

In 1503, Alexander, rumoured to have been poisoned, died from intestinal bleeding and fever. His corpse was so bloated it had to be forced inside the coffin. Four years later, Cesare died fighting in Spain and Lucrezia passed away in 1519 after complications in childbirth.

THE SPANISH INQUISITION

The Tribunal of the Holy Office of the Inquisition, known as the Spanish Inquisition, was founded in Spain in 1480 to combat heresy and root out apostates. It was feared for its zealous and often cruel defence of Catholic orthodoxy.

IN THE CELLS OF
THE SPANISH INQUISITION

When suspected apostates or heretics were arrested they were sent to jail for interrogation. Prisoners were frequently gagged and chained or left to sleep on filthy floors and starved. Troublesome suspects were punished with the *pie de amigo*, an iron fork that forced the head into an upright position. This was only a prelude to the most feared part of the process: the interrogation chamber. Ecclesiastical law forbade the Inquisition from bloodshed during an interrogation. But such was its fearsome reputation that it was often enough just to place the accused *conspectu tortorum* – 'in front of the instruments of torture' – to elicit a confession.

All suspects were stripped before the tortures began. Some might face the *garrucha*, a hanging by the wrists with heavy weights attached to the feet. Victims were raised slowly by a pulley system and then lowered until their limbs were dislocated. Others encountered the *potro*, which involved being bound to a rack with cords that were slowly tightened and bit into the flesh. But perhaps the most terrible method was the *toca*, a process akin to waterboarding. A victim was strapped to a slanted table and had strips of linen stuffed into his or her mouth. Jars of water were slowly poured over the face, nose, and throat to effect drowning.

Instruments of torture: the Spanish collar pierced the victim's neck while the rack stretched the limbs

THE *AUTO-DA-FÉ*

Victims may face a final humiliation at the hands of the Inquisition. The *autos-da-fé* ('acts of faith') were public trials that usually took place in town squares and drew huge crowds – a trial in Seville reportedly attracted 100,000. The accused was forced to don robes depicting their crimes and carry a tall mitre called a *coraza*. Some were punished by the *verguenza*, in which they were stripped to the waist and made to walk through the town bearing a symbol of their crime with a public crier before them. The most unfortunate faced death by burning. A pyre was constructed from charcoal, brushwood or faggots in the *quemadero*, on the outskirts of the town. The cause of death was often carbon monoxide poisoning or suffocation, but some were slowly and agonizingly burned alive.

THE *MALLEUS MALEFICARUM* AND THE WITCH CRAZE

First published in Germany in 1486, *Malleus Maleficarum* (*The Hammer of Witches*) inspired a horrific wave of persecution. The highly popular treatise, authored by inquisitors Heinrich Kramer and James Sprenger and licensed by the Catholic Church, went through fourteen editions by 1520. It focused predominently on women, arguing that they were more likely to practise witchcraft, and discussed the abilities of witches, as well as suitable punishments for them. It recommended subjects be stripped and shaved and their bodies examined for Devil's marks (a mark supposedly made by the Devil when the witch swore

The burning of witches

obedience). If the suspect did not volunteer a confession, she was to be interrogated and tortured. *Malleus Maleficarum* also advised that many witches were able to withstand long torture aided by the Devil. As such, interrogations of witches were lengthy. Suspects were routinely horsewhipped, and forced to drink 'witch broth' (a potion made from the ashes of burned witches) so they could not harm their interrogators. Their bodies were mutilated using red-hot pincers and irons, burning feathers dipped in sulphur, thumbscrews, and other

instruments such as the spider, a sharp metal fork used to mangle the breasts. The 'Witch Craze' swept across Europe, peaking in intensity during the late sixteenth and early seventeenth centuries. Tens of thousands of innocent women (and some men) were tortured and executed.

The spider, used to mangle the breasts

JOANNA THE MAD

Joanna was the third child of Ferdinand and Isabella, the monarchs who unified their separate realms of Aragon and Castile into one kingdom of Spain. In 1496, Joanna journeyed to Flanders to marry the Habsburg Duke of Burgundy, Philip the Fair. Their union would create one of the largest empires in world history and by 1498 both of Joanna's older siblings had died, leaving her as heir to Spain. Philip was constantly unfaithful, yet Joanna was devoted to him.

In 1502, Philip and Joanna travelled to Spain. When Philip returned home alone, he left a frantic Joanna attempting to escape her guarded apartments. When Joanna returned to Flanders in 1504, she humiliated herself when she saw a courtier flirting with Philip. Joanna flew at the woman, screaming insults, insisting a barber cut off the courtier's hair. Philip, furious, again confined his wife to her apartments. That November, Isabella died and in 1506 Joanna and Philip arrived in Spain to rule Castile. Joanna's father Ferdinand remained King of Aragon.

That September Philip developed a sudden fever and died. Joanna refused to leave her husband's embalmed corpse, and stayed by its side until it was entombed in a convent in Tordesillas, in central Spain. With Joanna unable to rule and her son Charles too young, Ferdinand became regent in Castile, and confined Joanna to the convent where her husband lay. Even when Joanna's son Charles became king of all Spain in 1516, Joanna remained in confinement. She became increasingly paranoid, frequently refusing to speak, eat, or bathe. Joanna was seemingly content to gaze at Philip's tomb and pray for his soul until her death in 1555.

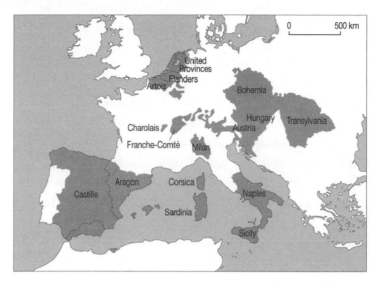

Unified Habsburg lands during the reign of Charles V

DEATH BY 1,000 CUTS

From 1505, Emperor Zhengde of the Ming Dynasty reigned over China. He was wholly devoted to pleasure – his harem was too large for his palace and he was content to let his court eunuchs handle the tedium of government. Eunuchs were important figures at the imperial court, acting as civil servants and officials.

The clique of eunuchs that dominated the court became known as the Eight Tigers. Their leader was Liu Jin. He had chosen to be castrated as a child so he could pursue a career at court and ascended the ranks quickly due to his sharp intellect and eloquence. Many resented Liu Jin's power and planned to depose him, but he brutally purged his enemies, meanwhile building up a sizeable fortune by embezzling imperial funds.

In 1510, Liu Jin's career met a brutal end. There were rumours he plotted to overthrow Zhengde and place a relative on the throne. Once a cache of weapons was found in Liu Jin's house, Zhengde had no choice but to sentence him to death using the cruellest method – the *lingchi*, or 'death by 1,000 cuts'. The victim was tied to a frame and, in a slow process, parts of his body were sliced off with knives. The practice continued even after the victim's death. Liu Jin's plotting was deemed so treasonous that his *lingchi* was to last three days. He died after two but it was still the longest *lingchi* ever carried out.

THE DEATH OF GYÖRGY DÓZSA

From the sixteenth to nineteenth centuries, Hungary bordered the Ottoman Empire. In 1514, the Pope initiated a Crusade against the Ottomans, promising freedom from serfdom to any peasants who agreed to fight. The nobility opposed this, and the Crusade was cancelled. The serfs, eager for freedom, staged an insurrection. Their leader was György Dózsa, a Hungarian soldier of fortune. After initial success, the peasant army was defeated by royal and noble forces. Dózsa was captured with other rebel leaders. Condemned to die, he was forced to sit on a heated iron throne and wear a white-hot iron crown. His comrades were ordered to both mutilate and devour his flesh. With Dózsa dead, the authorities were able to swiftly suppress the revolt.

MASSACRE OF THE FESTIVAL OF TOXCATL

In 1519, the leader of the Spanish conquistadors, Hernán Cortés, landed in Mexico with his army and advanced to the Aztec capital Tenochtitlan (the site of modern-day Mexico City). Emperor Moctezuma II welcomed him, providing a palace to garrison his troops. Eventually, however, tensions rose between the Aztecs and the Spanish and there were calls to evict Cortés. To forestall this, the Spaniard imprisoned Moctezuma. Meanwhile, the Spanish governor, who thought Cortés had exceeded his authority, sent a convoy to meet him. Now in command was Cortés's deputy, Pedro de Alvarado.

Moctezuma asked Alvarado for permission to hold Toxcatl, a religious festival. On 10 May, hundreds gathered in the main temple. Participants were richly dressed in pearls and precious stones and performed a ceremonial dance. Meanwhile, Alvarado arrived with several dozen soldiers and gave the order for his men to seal the exits. What followed was a massacre of hundreds. The first victim of the bloodbath was the drummer leading the dance, whose arms and head were cut off. Some Aztecs pretended to be dead, but as soon as they moved they were slaughtered. Conquistadors scoured the temple complex for hidden survivors, 'as the smell of blood and entrails fouled the air'.

Some believe Alvarado was preventing an uprising against the Spanish, others that he coveted the rich costumes of the Aztecs. The massacre resulted in a popular backlash that forced the Spanish out of Tenochtitlan, but that August they returned to ultimately capture the city.

THE STOCKHOLM BLOODBATH

In 1520, Sweden was split between those who favoured union with Denmark and those who opposed it. That year, Christian II of Denmark invaded and in November he was crowned king in Stockholm. Those who had opposed him were promised amnesty and many were invited to dine with the new king. It was a ruse to capture them. Eighty-two people, including bishops, nobles, and civic officials, were hanged or beheaded. Their bodies were burned en masse.

But the massacre backfired. The Swedish populace were horrified at the violence and rose up in support of an influential noble called Gustavus Vasa. After a two-year war with Christian, Vasa was proclaimed king in 1523. He went on to lead Sweden to independence and it became a nation of considerable influence in Europe.

MAGELLAN'S LAST STAND

Ferdinand Magellan led the Spanish expedition that completed the first circumnavigation of the globe. In March 1521, the expedition reached Cebu in the Philippines. Magellan befriended an influential chieftain, who converted to Catholicism and ordered other local leaders to do the same. The only rebel was Lapu-Lapu, a chief on nearby Mactan Island.

Magellan's men sacked Lapu-Lapu's capital and ordered him to pay tribute. When Lapu-Lapu refused to pay the full amount,

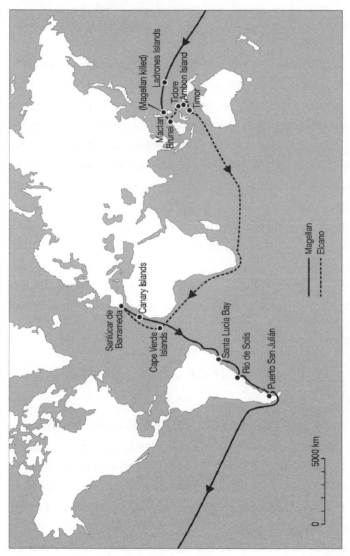

Circumnavigation of the globe: Magellan's journey

Magellan and forty-eight men sailed to Mactan on a punitive expedition. Awaiting them were Lapu-Lapu's army of 1,500. As Magellan advanced, Lapu-Lapu retreated, drawing the attackers inland. Magellan, realizing they were imperilled, ordered a general retreat. While he and eight of his men remained ashore to assist the evacuation, Magellan was wounded in the leg by a poisoned arrow. Once his men had reached their boats, Magellan agreed to retreat – he had to be carried because of his injury. Then, Lapu-Lapu's warriors launched a determined attack on Magellan, showering him with spears, stones, and clods of earth. Magellan was wounded in the face and lost his lance in the body of one of his attackers. Lapu-Lapu's men swamped him, killing him with cutlasses and bamboo spears. Magellan's body was never recovered.

After the battle, the expedition – led by Juan Sebastián Elcano, Magellan's second in command – left the Philippines and arrived in Spain in September 1522.

THE SACK OF ROME

In 1524, Pope Clement VII was fearful of the growing power of the Habsburg Charles V (King Charles I of Spain) who ruled over a vast realm including Spain, the Low Countries, Naples and Sicily, as well as being Holy Roman Emperor, which made him overlord of Germany. Clement feared Charles would dominate all Italy, and allied against him with France, Milan, Venice, and Florence. Resistance to Charles proved futile and his army defeated all those who stood against them.

However, Charles's resources were stretched and by 1527 he was unable to pay his multinational army, which even included Lutheran Germans. The army revolted and forced their commander, Charles de Bourbon, to lead them to Rome so they could recoup their losses by sacking the city. On 6 May, 20,000 mutinous soldiers attacked Rome, vastly outnumbering the city's garrison of 8,000. Though Bourbon died in the attack, Rome's defences were breached. The Pope's Swiss Guard heroically defended St Peter's Basilica, giving the Pope time to flee to his fortress on the outskirts of Rome, the Castel Sant'Angelo.

The sack was more brutal than any before it. The mutineers killed all they met. Citizens were cruelly tortured so they would reveal the location of buried treasure. At St Peter's, 500 were killed on the high altar. Palaces and churches were ransacked, papal tombs were violated, and holy relics destroyed. The head of St Andrew was thrown to the ground. One soldier attached a piece of the Holy Lance (that which pierced Christ's side as he hung on the cross) to his spear and paraded it through the streets. The Lutherans used St Peter's to stable their horses. The carnage did not stop until 10 May. One thousand soldiers and 25,000 civilians lay dead.

In June, the Pope surrendered to the Habsburgs. Although the sack was a source of shame for the devout Charles, it played into his hands, as it left him the dominant power in Italy and with a pope in his thrall.

THE EATEN EXPLORER

Giovanni da Verrazzano was an Italian explorer who won French sponsorship to search for the Northwest Passage, a sea route that connected the Atlantic and Pacific Oceans. During his first voyage in 1524, Verrazzano explored the Carolina coast, before sailing up to Newfoundland. His search for the Passage was fruitless. The following year he journeyed to Brazil and returned with a valuable cargo of brazilwood, a prized timber. In 1528, he launched his final expedition, exploring Florida and the Bahamas before anchoring near an island (thought to be Guadalupe) and rowing ashore. Before his stunned crew could respond, a group of the native Caribs attacked, killed and ate him.

THE MÜNSTER REBELLION

In 1517, Martin Luther published *Ninety-Five Theses*, igniting the Protestant Reformation, which flourished in the Holy Roman Empire. Dozens of new sects were formed, the most radical of which were the Anabaptists (so-called because they practised adult baptism). Most of the empire's components were virtually independent, and many chose to follow Protestantism. One such place was the city of Münster, in north-west Germany, which despite being nominally ruled by a Catholic bishop, officially became Lutheran in 1533.

However, Münster was near to the Netherlands, a hotbed of Anabaptism. Adherents of this sect began to dominate the city and in 1534 two Dutchmen, Jan Matthys and Jan Bockelsen, seized power. Münster became a theocracy. It was proclaimed that the

Earth was doomed and only Münster would be saved. Catholics and Lutherans were evicted and it became a capital offence not to follow Anabaptism. Citizens were forced to surrender cash and valuables. All books, save the Bible, were burned.

Meanwhile, the Catholic bishop had hired an army to besiege Münster. In March, Matthys was killed, leaving Bockelsen as leader. He proclaimed himself king, established polygamy (taking fifteen wives), and made even minor offences such as quarrelling capital crimes. However, the bishop's army began to intensify their siege, blockading Münster, which led to mass starvation. In June, they launched a surprise attack and took the town. Bockelsen was captured, and paraded around the region in chains. In January 1536, he and two other leaders were returned to Münster to be publically tortured to death by red-hot irons. Their mangled corpses were suspended in cages from a church tower. The cages still hang today, although the bodies have long since decomposed.

HENRY VIII AND THE CHURCH OF ENGLAND

Henry VIII became king in 1509 and married his brother's widow Catherine of Aragon. At this time Henry was every inch the dashing Renaissance prince: composer, scholar, and keen sportsman. The problem was his wife. By 1519, the King of France noted that while Henry was still 'young and handsome' he had an 'old, deformed wife'. More importantly for Henry, after five pregnancies only one (female) child had survived infancy. Henry craved a son, and by the late 1520s was besotted with Anne Boleyn who, unlike most women the king desired, would not submit to his amorous advances unless they married.

Henry needed a divorce, which required a papal annulment, so he could marry Anne. Unfortunately for Henry, Catherine's nephew, Emperor Charles V, had complete control of the Pope after the Sack of Rome, making the annulment impossible. In 1532, Parliament passed an act making Henry the supreme head of the Church of England and separating the country from Rome. Henry was now able to divorce Catherine and marry Anne.

ANNE'S BEHEADING

For all their differences, Catherine and Anne had a fatal similarity: only providing Henry with daughters. In January 1536, Anne suffered a second miscarriage. The foetus was thought to have been male. Henry took this as a sign that his marriage to Anne was doomed. Within weeks she was accused of adultery and incest, imprisoned in the Tower of London and sentenced to death. Her five alleged lovers, including her brother, were executed. A French

Anne was imprisoned in the Tower of London

swordsman was imported so Anne would not face the commoner's axe. He beheaded her with a single stroke.

THE CONQUEST OF THE INCAS

The Inca Empire covered much of western South America, centring on its capital Cusco, in modern Peru. Civil war and smallpox crippled the empire. In 1533, Francisco Pizarro, a Spanish conquistador, took advantage of this and entered Inca territory, capturing and executing the emperor Atahualpa. He faced revolt from Manco Inca, whom Pizarro had installed as a puppet ruler of the Inca. Despite gathering an army of 200,000, Manco was unable to dislodge Pizarro. In 1539, the Spanish captured Manco's sister-wife Cura Ocllo. She was marched to Cusco and en route forced to witness the execution of some of her brothers. Guards repeatedly tried to rape her, so she covered her body in 'filthy matter' to deter them. Eventually she was stripped and tied to a stake, then beaten and shot to death with arrows. Her body was floated down the Yucay River in a basket to be found by her husband. Manco was killed in 1544 – his revolt was the last widespread effort to dislodge the Spanish.

THE ASSASSINATION OF
FRANCISCO PIZARRO

Pizarro, ruling as governor, faced opposition from Diego de Almagro, a former companion who wanted a greater share in the riches of the conquest. Almagro and his faction had captured Cusco in 1537, but Pizarro defeated them the following year and Almagro

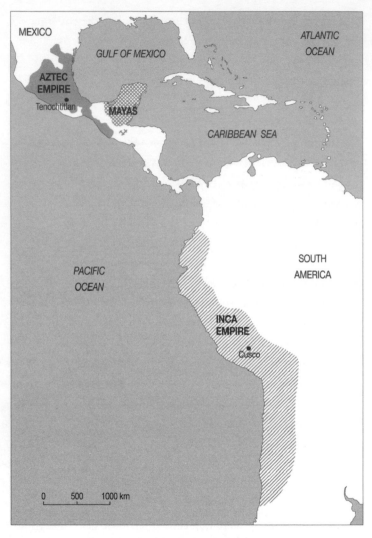

Pre-Columbian Central and South America

was executed. Almagro's supporters, including his son Diego II, swore vengeance. In 1541, a group of them surprised Pizarro in his palace in Lima. Pizarro managed to strap on some armour and kill one of his assailants but he was overwhelmed and stabbed to death. Diego II proclaimed himself governor but was unable to hold on to power. He was captured and executed in 1542 by Cristóbal Vaca de Castro, the new governor sent by Spain, who successfully restored order.

TSAR IVAN IV OF RUSSIA

Ivan the Terrible became the Grand Prince of Moscow in 1533 at the age of three when his father Vasili III died of blood poisoning. Ivan was content to let his mother Elena Glinskaya act as regent, while he engaged in other pursuits. It is said he enjoyed throwing animals from high towers to witness their destruction. So disdainful was Ivan of affairs of state that when a delegation of citizens came to petition him he grew enraged and poured boiling wine on them. He then made them undress, lie on the ground and wait for execution – fortunately for them, Ivan was called away and forgot about putting them to death.

IVAN BECOMES 'TERRIBLE'

In the 1550s, Ivan began to impose his will on Russia, igniting a war with the Polish-Lithuanian Commonwealth (a union of the Kingdom of Poland and the Grand Duchy of Lithuania) and Sweden, and beginning to extend his personal authority. The agent of his rule was a fearsome secret police force called the *oprichniki*. Ivan's main targets were Russia's noble families, which he saw as a threat to his absolute rule.

In 1567, Ivan confiscated and then ravaged the lands of Petrovich Federov, an influential noble. The inhabitants of one of his estates

Ivan the Terrible

were forced into their houses, below which Ivan's men ignited barrels of gunpowder. The grand prince delighted in watching their bodies being blasted into the air. The following year Federov was summoned to court in Moscow. Ivan ordered him to don royal garments and sit on his throne. Ivan then knelt before Federov and said, 'Since I have the power to seat you, I can also unseat you,' before plunging a knife into his heart. Ivan's soldiers then stabbed Federov in the stomach, pulling out his entrails.

In 1569, the Lithuanians made inroads into Russian territory. Believing that the nobles in the city of Novgorod were treasonous and planning to defect to Lithuania, Ivan was determined to root them out. In 1570, he led an army into the region. First he ravaged the area round Tver, killing 36,000. Double that number died of starvation and disease. In Novgorod, Ivan's men killed hundreds of members of the noble families, as well as hundreds of citizens. At least 2,000 died. Some were bound together, thrown into holes in the frozen river and left to drown or freeze to death.

In 1581, Ivan fell into a quarrel with his son, the tsarevich Ivan. The elder had found his son's pregnant wife in the palace, wearing what he saw as immodest clothing. He had beaten her, causing her to miscarry. The younger Ivan angrily confronted his father and their argument escalated until, it is alleged, the tsar struck his son in the head with his sceptre, causing the wound that led to his death.

Ivan the Terrible died of a stroke in 1584, leaving his sickly, possibly mentally ill and childless son Feodor as tsar. Feodor died in 1598, plunging Russia into a decade of famine and unrest known as the 'Time of Troubles'.

POPE JULIUS III AND THE TEENAGE CARDINAL

Pope Julius III was elected in 1550. He proved an ineffectiual pope: erratic, moody, and devoted to his own pleasure. He was also notorious for his relationship with Innocenzo, a youth from Parma, who was legally adopted by Julius's brother. There had been whispers Julius was a sodomite since the 1540s, and it was rumoured Innocenzo shared his bed. When Julius became pope he made the seventeen-year-old boy a cardinal and showered him with lucrative offices. Julius died in 1555 and Innocenzo was treated with disdain because of his dissolute ways. He was accused of rape, murder and kidnapping, but escaped serious punishment. He died in 1577.

THE JOUST THAT IGNITED THE FRENCH WARS OF RELIGION

In the mid-sixteenth century, Protestantism was on the rise in France, particularly among the nobility. King Henry II of France, however, was a fierce defender of Catholicism, and Calvinists, known as Huguenots, faced harsh persecution at the hands of his regime.

In 1551, Henry was at war with the Habsburgs – rulers of Spain, the Low Countries, and most of Italy – and sought to dislodge them as the dominant force in Europe. The two powers made peace in 1559 and Henry's daughter Elizabeth was to marry King Philip II of Spain, the widowed husband of Mary I of England. A tournament was held near Paris to celebrate the union.

On 30 June, Henry entered the tournament. He was an avid jouster but had recently suffered from vertigo. After two successful tilts, Henry faced Gabriel Montgomery, a captain in his Scots Guard. Montgomery almost unhorsed Henry but the king insisted on another tilt. They clashed and Montgomery's lance drove splinters into Henry's forehead – his visor had flown open during the joust. The king reeled, bleeding profusely. Barely moving, he was carried into his palace where the best physicians in France were called to attend him. For a brief moment it seemed Henry might recover. However, by 8 July his condition had worsened. The physicians considered trepanning Henry's skull, but when they removed his bandages there was so much pus that the situation was hopeless.

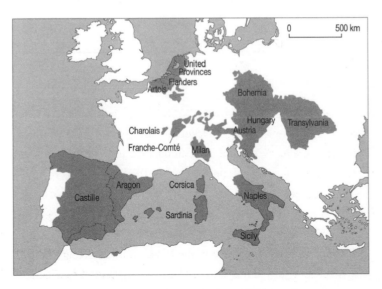

The Habsburg Empire in 1551

Henry died on 10 July. The new king, his son Francis, was a sickly fifteen-year-old completely unable to impose central royal authority and deal with the growing religious factionalism in France. Francis died in 1560, succeeded by his ten-year-old brother, Charles. Armed conflict broke out in 1562 and lasted intermittently until 1598, costing the lives of tens of thousands and devastating France.

THE SIEGE OF NICOSIA

Cyprus had been part of the Venetian Republic since the late fifteenth century and remained so until the Ottomans arrived in 1570. The Ottoman army landed in July and by the end of the month had surrounded Nicosia, the island's capital. They battered the city with a continuous cannonade of arrow-, musket- and cannon-fire. On 9 September, after a sustained attack, the Ottomans breached the city walls. Italian merchants and officials were put to the sword while cannonballs were fired at a crowd in the main square. Nicosia was looted and as many as 20,000 were killed. Cyprus remained part of the Ottoman Empire until the nineteenth century.

The
Early Modern Era

c. AD 1570 to 1700

THE ST BARTHOLOMEW'S DAY
MASSACRES

IN 1559, WARS of Religion beset France. The reign of sickly
Francis II lasted less than eighteen months and he was
succeeded by his brother, Charles IX. As Charles was a minor
the Queen Mother, Italian Catherine de' Medici, served as regent.
She became one of the most powerful people in the kingdom.

In 1570, peace between Catholics and Huguenots was
negotiated. One of the conditions was the marriage of the Huguenot
Henry of Navarre (ruler of a small kingdom in southern France,
and also third in line to the throne), to Margaret of Valois, the
younger sister of King Charles. The hard-line Catholic faction, led
by the influential Guise family, refused to accept the peace.

On 18 August 1572, the marriage of Margaret and Navarre took place in Paris, bringing the most important nobles of all faiths to the capital. On 22 August, there was an assassination attempt on Gaspard de Coligny, the Huguenot political leader. The Huguenot response to the attempt was furious – so much so that it led to rumours that they secretly planned to seize the royal family and eliminate Huguenot enemies at court.

Charles and Medici, in league with the Guises, ordered a pre-emptive strike on the Huguenot leadership on 23 August, the eve of St Bartholomew's Day. The following day, a group of Guise men surprised Coligny at his lodgings in Paris. He was killed and his body tossed out of a window. Youths mutilated Coligny's corpse and dragged it through the streets. They then conducted a mock trial of the corpse, burned it and slung it into the River Seine. Coligny's charred body was later recovered from the water and hung from the common gallows.

Meanwhile, members of the king's guard patrolled through the streets of Paris seeking to eliminate other leading Huguenots. Word quickly spread among the Parisian people of the purge and many took it as a chance to kill their Huguenot neighbours. Even the city militia, stationed to keep order, joined in the slaughter. Bonfires were made of Protestant books and killers forced their victims to recant their faith and repeat Catholic prayers, or face death. In a gruesome parody of religious ceremony, infants were 'baptized' in the blood of their parents. Foetuses were cut from the wombs of their mothers, and plunged into the Seine. Looting, pillaging, and extortion accompanied the bloodbath.

Over the weeks that followed, violence against Huguenots spread across France. Around 3,000 were killed in Paris and a similar

The St Bartholomew's Day Massacre

number in the rest of the country. At first Charles claimed the Guises were responsible for the massacre but once he realized its popularity he claimed public credit. The massacre devastated the Huguenot leadership and many of their number emigrated.

War restarted, with the Catholics claiming the ascendancy. Navarre narrowly escaped death by converting to Catholicism and became a virtual prisoner at court. But when King Charles died in 1574 and was succeeded by his brother Henry III, Navarre escaped court and rejoined the Huguenot cause as leader, spurring them to success in the wars that followed.

THE ASSASSINATION OF WILLIAM OF ORANGE

Prince William of Orange was the figurehead of the Dutch struggle for independence from the Spanish Habsburgs. Desperate to put an end to the revolt, Philip II of Spain had placed a 25,000 *écu* price on William's head. So rich a bounty attracted many would-be assassins before the successful attempt.

In 1582, a young clerk Jean Jauréguy surprised William while he was dining, levelled a pistol at his head and pulled the trigger. Being inexperienced, however, Jauréguy had overloaded his pistol and blew off his own hand. The bullet did hit William, although it entered his cheek and palate without striking a bone or vital organ. William's guards stabbed Jauréguy to death before he could be questioned.

In the summer of 1584, Balthasar Gérard, a cabinet-maker's apprentice from Spanish-controlled Franche-Comté (in modern-day eastern France), arrived at William's residence in Delft. On 10

July, he saw an opportunity to strike. Despite the threats to his safety, William kept an open court so he could receive petitioners and Gérard joined the crowd. When William was walking to his dining room, Gérard fired at him with a heavy double-barrelled pistol. Two slugs entered William's lungs and stomach, plastering the walls with his blood. William staggered forward, uttering, 'My God, have pity on my soul; my God, have pity on this poor people.' His sister asked him if he was reconciled with Jesus Christ and William, with his every last effort, answered yes. He then lost consciousness, dying before his physician could arrive.

The assassination of Orange

William did not die in vain. The Dutch went on to achieve full independence from Spain in 1648 and William was venerated as the founder of a nation.

THE EXECUTION OF BALTHASAR GÉRARD

Gérard was captured attempting to vault a garden wall while fleeing William's palace. He was seized and willingly confessed to his crime; after a brief trial, he was sentenced to die. Gérard was brutally tortured. First, he was hung on a pole and flayed. Heavy weights were attached to his toes and he was forced to wear tight leather shoes too. His feet were then placed near a fire, which made the shoes contract and crush his toes. When the shoes were ripped off, so too was his skin. Boiling fat was poured over him and sharp nails driven into his hands and feet.

Gérard was executed on 14 July. His right hand was burned off and his flesh torn with pincers in six places. He was then quartered and disembowelled and his heart was flung in his face. Finally, he was beheaded. Gérard prayed in a low voice throughout his ordeal while the baying crowds revelled at his suffering.

Gérard's family did receive a reward for his deed: Philip II granted them estates in their native Franche-Comté.

THE WEREWOLF OF BEDBURG

In the late sixteenth century, the town of Bedburg in western Germany was the site of many violent murders. Hunters apprehended the killer in 1589. Peter Stumpp was a local farmer, who claimed to have been a werewolf for over a quarter of a century.

Under torture on the rack, Stumpp revealed the gruesome nature of the murders. He claimed that when he was twelve he had been seduced by the Devil who had given him a belt with the power to transform him into a werewolf. In this form, Stumpp craved blood. His first victims were lambs and kids, which he would kill and eat while they were still warm. He eventually moved on to human victims. He murdered at least thirteen youths and

Peter Stumpp, broken on the wheel and beheaded

two pregnant women, feasting on their bodies as well as those of the unborn foetuses. It was rumoured he had also murdered his son and eaten his brains. After his wife's death, Stumpp had incestuous relations with his daughter, Sybil, as well as his cousin, Trompin.

Stumpp was sentenced to death. His daughter and cousin were also arrested as accomplices and were strangled and burned. Stumpp was condemned to be broken on the wheel. He was bound, spreadeagled, to the spokes and red-hot pincers were used to remove his flesh. A wooden hatchet was used to break his arms and legs. He was then beheaded and burned.

THE TIME OF TROUBLES

Ivan the Terrible was succeeded by his feeble son Fyodor in 1584 and Boris Godunov, a prominent member of the regency council, become de facto head of state. One of Boris's first acts was to force

Ivan's youngest son Tsarevich Dmitri, whose supporters were calling for to replace Fyodor, into exile. In 1591, news spread that Dmitri had been killed.

In 1598, the childless Fyodor died. With no heir, a national assembly was called, which elected Godunov the new tsar. He purged his enemies, including the influential Shuisky and Romanov families. Famine beset Godunov's reign. In 1601, heavy rains and cold weather destroyed the grain crop. The following year an early winter ruined the harvest. Food prices rocketed, and Russia began to starve. The people were forced to eat hay, grass, bark and roots – before moving on to horses, dogs, cats and even humans. The poor were so starved that they were forced to sell themselves into slavery, or turn to begging or banditry. In 1604, good harvests returned, but the famine had killed one-third of the population.

TSAR DMITRI THE FALSE?

In 1600 in Moscow, a man emerged claiming to be the tsarevich Dmitri, who had been presumed dead for nearly a decade. He fled to Poland before Godunov could capture him. Some doubted Dmitri's claims, believing that he was a bastard son of the Polish king or a runaway monk. Nevertheless Dmitri, with support from Godunov's enemies and Poland, invaded Russia in 1604. The ensuing civil war saw large areas of the country razed and plundered.

Godunov died in April 1605 and was succeeded by his son Fyodor. That June, Dmitri's supporters strangled Fyodor II to death and Dmitri entered Moscow to be crowned tsar. However, his subsequent marriage to a Polish Catholic noblewoman incited fury and Dmitri made many enemies in the Russian Orthodox Church. His adversaries were led by powerful nobleman Vasili Shuisky.

On 17 May 1606, Vasili's men raided the Kremlin at dawn, forcing their way into Dmitri's chambers. The tsar attempted to jump out of a window to safety but slipped and fell, breaking his leg. The raiders shot the incapacitated Dmitri and then hacked him to death. He was stripped naked and dragged out to Red Square by cords tied to his legs and genitals. He was laid out with a minstrel's bagpipe in his mouth and a mask on his belly, signifying that he was an imposter. Dmitri's body remained there for three days before it was burned.

THE BLOOD COUNTESS

Elizabeth Báthory was born in 1560 to a noble Hungarian family. Aged fifteen she married Ferencz Nádasdy, an important general. He was frequently away on campaign, so Elizabeth was left in charge of their castle in Čachtice (in modern-day Slovakia). Her rule over the household was brutal.

Servant girls were beaten and their lips pierced with pins. If Elizabeth's ruff was laundered or starched improperly, red-hot irons were pressed onto the feet and mouths of the offending maids. Torture became murder. Victims were dragged naked in the snow and had water poured onto them until they froze to death. One servant girl was stripped, covered with honey and left overnight to be stung and bitten by insects.

After her husband died in 1604, Elizabeth's cruelty knew no limits. Her accomplices scoured the countryside for new servant girls and daughters of the gentry were invited to live in her castle. A contemporary letter records, 'at least 300 girls and women, nobly born as well as commoners … were put to death in an inhuman and cruel manner. She cut their flesh and made them grill it; afterwards she would make them eat bits of their own bodies.'

Eventually Elizabeth's activities drew the attention of the authorities. She was placed on trial in 1611 and found guilty. The court deemed her acts 'satanic terror against Christian blood … horrifying cruelties unheard of among the female sex since the world begun'. As she was of noble blood, Elizabeth was not executed. Rather, she was placed under lifelong house arrest in the castle where she had committed her foul deeds.

MASSACRE AT SEA: THE BATTLE OF GIBRALTAR

Having recovered from the death of William of Orange, the Dutch continued to defy Spain. They were particularly successful at sea and, in 1607, launched a daring raid on a Spanish fleet anchored in the Bay of Gibraltar. All twenty-one Spanish ships were either disabled or destroyed. The Dutch lost not a single vessel, although their admiral died of his injuries after a cannonball severed his leg. With the situation hopeless, the Spanish surrendered. The Dutch refused to accept and sent men out in boats to the ruined Spanish ships. They rowed among the devastated fleet, shooting and stabbing any survivors they found in the water. At least 2,000 Spaniards died in the battle and ensuing massacre.

THE ASSASSINATION
OF HENRY IV

In 1589, Henry of Navarre succeeded his distant relative Henry III
as King of France. The powerful and staunchly Catholic Guise family
opposed the succession and the French Wars of Religion continued.
In 1593, Navarre converted to Catholicism, stating that 'Paris is well
worth a Mass'. By 1598, he had defeated his enemies and brought
peace to France. He granted toleration for Huguenots, earning him
the enmity of some Catholics.

On 14 May 1610, Henry journeyed from the Tuileries Palace to
the Bastille to meet his chief minister, the Duke of Sully. The royal
carriage, protected by armed horsemen and guards, travelled
through the narrow Parisian streets. Watching Henry's movements
was François Ravaillac. He was a legal functionary and devout
Catholic who fervently hated Huguenots. When Henry's guards left
the royal coach to investigate a blockage in the road Ravaillac jumped
on the wheel closest to Henry, brandishing a blade. His first blow cut
across Henry's chest; the second pierced his lung and severed his
aorta and vena cava. Henry said, 'It's nothing,' before slumping over
dead, blood pouring from his mouth. Ravaillac was seized and on 27
May, in front of a baying mob, he was tied to four horses and torn
to pieces.

ABBAS, SAFI, AND
THE SAFAVID DYNASTY

The Safavid Dynasty won control of the Persian Empire in the early sixteenth century, ruling over a realm that covered much of modern Iran, Azerbaijan, Armenia, and Iraq, as well as stretching into the Caucasus and Pakistan. The dynasty's greatest shah (king) was Abbas I, who deposed his father Mohammad I in 1587. Abbas banished his father and two brothers, whom he had blinded. While Abbas was an able ruler, successfully transforming the military and government, he was also extremely suspicious. In 1615, he ordered the death of his

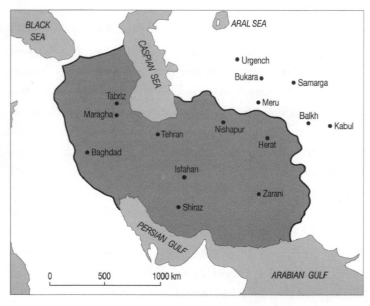

The Safavid Empire 1501–1723

own son after unfounded rumours that he had plotted to overthrow him. Abbas was succeeded by his eighteen-year-old grandson, Shah Safi I, since his sons and brothers had been killed or blinded.

In the early years of Safi's reign, any perceived rivals were systematically slaughtered, including royal princes who had already been blinded during Abbas's reign. With his purges complete, Safi, unprepared for controlling the centralized government his grandfather had built and largely uneducated, was content to let his underlings rule. The Persian Empire slowly lost territory to its neighbours. An opium addict with a taste for wine, Safi died suddenly in 1642. He was succeeded by his more capable son, Abbas II.

THE SACK OF MAGDEBURG

The Thirty Years' War began in 1618. It was largely a religious conflict between Protestants and Catholics in the Holy Roman Empire, but it eventually drew in most of Europe's major powers. In 1630, King Gustavus Adolphus of Sweden had entered the war in support of the Protestants, giving their cause a major boost. That December Magdeburg, an important Protestant city in eastern-central Germany with a population of 25,000, was under siege by a Catholic imperial army.

In April 1631, the imperial general, Count Tilly, took command of the siege, hoping to draw Gustavus to the interior of the country. By May, Tilly's army had captured the suburbs. Gustavus was unable to reach the city but Magdeburg refused to surrender. On 20 May, the imperial army breached the city's inner defences. The ensuing sack was the greatest single tragedy of a brutal war. Imperial soldiers ravaged the city, raping and pillaging as they went. Fires quickly spread, burning and suffocating thousands.

There were too many corpses to bury so they were tossed into the nearby Elbe River. Around 20,000 citizens and defenders died during the sack. By 1632, only 449 people lived in Magdeburg and even by the early eighteenth century large areas remained in ruins.

THE WITCHFINDER GENERAL

The English Civil War between the supporters of Parliament and King Charles I began in 1642. During the war, a lawyer called Matthew Hopkins came to prominence as a witchfinder. For a fee, he and his assistant John Stearne would root out witches in East Anglia and the neighbouring counties. His first victim was an innocent one-legged woman called Elizabeth Clark, whom Hopkins tortured until she confessed to sleeping with the Devil. Taking advantage of the general paranoia arising from the upheavals of war, Hopkins was successful in twisting suspicion into accusation and his methods for forcing confessions were staggeringly cruel. He beat, starved and denied sleep to his suspects, making them pace back and forth in their cells until their feet blistered. In this state, they were forced to admit they had signed pacts with the Devil. Women were also thrown into water in a process known as 'swimming' – if they floated they were witches. Around 300 women were hanged as a result of Hopkins's baseless accusations. By 1646, Hopkins had begun to attract criticism for his use of torture and increasingly high fees. He faded into obscurity and, according to Stearne, died in 1647 after 'a long sicknesse of consumption'.

THE TEN-DAY MASSACRE

The Qing Dynasty was established in Beijing in 1644 but remnants loyal to the previous Ming regime still remained in southern China. The Qing leader Prince Dodo sought to bring them to heel. His first objective was the city of Yangzhou. Shi Kefa, the commander of the city, refused to surrender to Dodo's forces. After five days of bitter struggle, the Qing soldiers broke through Yangzhou's defences. Shi Kefa knew his resistance was hopeless, writing in his last letter, 'Death is surely my destiny.' Once captured, he was brought before Dodo and asked to submit for a final time. He again refused and was executed. His body was never recovered. Then, the once-magnificent Yangzhou was virtually wiped off the map.

First the Qing set the city aflame. Many burned to death in their houses, leaving only charred remains. The citizens were powerless to resist. An eyewitness reported, 'None dared to flee, but each stretched out his neck, expecting the stroke of the sword.' Some attempted suicide to escape the onslaught. The soldiers spared no one: 'the ground was stained with blood and covered with mutilated and dismembered bodies'. After ten days of slaughter, the city was in ruins. Estimates of casualties vary, but it is probable that at least 300,000 people died at the hands of Prince Dodo's men.

THE EXECUTION OF CHARLES I

After nearly seven years of civil war the Royalists had been defeated and their leader Charles I was captive at the hands of Parliment. Charles was put on trial in January 1649. He remained defiant. After a week he was condemned 'a tyrant, traitor, murderer and a public enemy', and sentenced to death. At 10 a.m. on 30 January, Charles was brought to a room in Whitehall overlooking the scaffold. The execution was delayed and it was rumoured that no executioner could be found. Some alleged that Oliver Cromwell, the military leader who had helped to overthrow the Stuart monarchy, stepped in. This is unlikely. The executioner was almost certainly the expert

The execution of Charles I

London hangman Richard Brandon and the delay probably came from his trouble in finding an assistant. Both Brandon and his assistant were masked and wore wigs and false beards so their identities would remain secret. At 2 p.m. Charles was brought to the scaffold. He had worn a doublet and cloak so he would not shiver in the cold, lest it be mistaken for fear. In his last speech he declared himself a 'martyr of the people'. He then tucked his hair into a cap and laid his neck on the block. His head was removed in a single blow and the crowd groaned. Some spectators lingered to dip their handkerchiefs in the king's blood. No English monarch had been put on trial and condemned before. England was no longer a kingdom, but a republic.

MASSACRE AT DROGHEDA

In August 1649, Oliver Cromwell led 15,000 men across the Irish Sea, landing in Dublin.

An alliance of Irish Catholics and Royalists remained in rebellion and Cromwell was determined to destroy them. His first target was Drogheda, a strategically vital port 28 miles north of Dublin. Drogheda was well defended, with walls 6 feet deep and 20 feet tall, sturdy towers and outworks and a garrison of 3,000.

Cromwell planned to storm the town after bombarding it with heavy artillery. He gave the garrison commander Sir Arthur Aston the chance to surrender. Aston refused, so on 10 September Cromwell began his artillery assault. The walls were breached the following day. Almost all the garrison was massacred, as well as numerous civilians. Aston was beaten to death with his own wooden leg. When some Royalist troops took shelter in a church steeple, Cromwell ordered his men to pile pews underneath and set them on fire. The men either burned to death or were cut down in flight. The Catholic clergy were slaughtered. Cromwell called the massacre 'a righteous judgment of God'.

By 1653, Parliament had crushed all opposition in Ireland, and the country became a Commonwealth with England, Wales, and Scotland. Cromwell was Lord Protector, the ruler of the British Isles. He died in 1658. Without his force of personality the Commonwealth fell apart, and the monarchy was restored under Charles II in 1660.

THE MASSACRE OF THE VAUDOIS

The Vaudois (also known as the Waldensians) were a radical Christian group condemned as heretics by the Catholic Church in the twelfth century. In 1655, the ruler of Piedmont in north-west Italy, Duke Charles Emmanuel II of the Savoy, ordered the Vaudois to convert to Catholicism or relocate to the upper valleys within twenty days on pain of death. Having heard reports of Vaudois resistance, the duke ordered a general massacre on 24 April. The fortunate were shot, stoned, or cut down with swords. Others were stripped naked, tightly bound with their heads between their legs, and rolled down a precipice to their death. Some had their mouths stuffed with gunpowder, which was then ignited. Children were torn from their parents' arms and dashed against the rocks. The sick and old were burned alive in their houses. Women and girls were raped and then impaled on pikes. The precise death toll is unknown but so brutal was the massacre that it attracted indignation across Europe.

LA QUINTRALA

In the seventeenth century, Chile was part of the Spanish Habsburg Empire. Dona Catalina de los Ríos y Lísperguer, who was known as 'La Quintrala' for her red hair, lived north of Santiago. Born in 1604, she had inherited a large estate after allegedly murdering her father by feeding him poisoned chicken. She commanded her tenants, slaves and servants with ruthless authority and all she deemed lazy were victims of her bouts of psychosis. La Quintrala used shackles, clamps, gags, and rawhide whips to brutally discipline her charges. One female servant accused of incivility was bound to a chair, beaten until bloody, and thrown into a freezing stream. Others were burned alive. While such savagery was normally reserved for her inferiors, on one occasion she stabbed an influential gentleman with whom she was romantically involved. The crime was blamed on a servant, who was executed.

In 1665, La Quintrala was finally made to answer for her crimes and tried in Santiago. She was accused of killing at least forty servants. Despite bribing witnesses, she was found guilty. However, as she had fallen ill, she escaped execution and was sentenced to house arrest in Santiago. She died later that year.

THE GREAT FIRE OF EDO

In 1657, a horrific fire struck the Japanese capital of Edo (now known as Tokyo), the greatest conflagration to hit the city until the bombings of World War II. The fire began on 2 March and lasted three days. Since most of the city's houses were made from wood and paper, the fire spread rapidly in the strong winds. It completely destroyed three-quarters of the city's buildings and killed one-seventh of the city's population of 600,000. When the last flames were extinguished, the dead were collected and buried in mass graves.

ENGLAND'S MOST INCOMPETENT EXECUTIONER

Jack Ketch was London's common hangman from 1666, overseeing the eight annual hanging days on the western outskirts of the city at Tyburn Gallows (near present-day Marble Arch). During the turbulent reign of King Charles II, Ketch attained infamy as an inept headsman. Charles had no legitimate children, so his heir was his Catholic brother James. This was unacceptable to many Protestants, who coalesced into a faction known as the Whigs. In 1683, Ketch was called to execute Lord William Russell, who had been involved in a failed plot to assassinate Charles and James. Ketch took three swings of his axe and still failed to take off Russell's head. He finished the job with a saw. Ketch blamed Russell for the debacle, claiming Russell's refusal to wear a blindfold caused him to flinch when the axe was swung, which ruined the stroke.

In 1685, Charles died and was succeeded by the Catholic James II. Charles's bastard son the Duke of Monmouth launched a revolt, but was defeated and sentenced to die. Ketch was to be his executioner. Aware of Ketch's reputation, Monmouth tipped him in the hope it would bring a speedy execution. But Ketch's axe was blunt. After three blows Monmouth was still not dead. Exhausted, Ketch threw down his axe. The crowd howled for him to finish the job. After two further blows, Monmouth's head remained attached and Ketch had to finish the job with a knife. So furious were the crowds, guards had to escort Ketch away to preserve his safety.

Ketch died in 1687. His name was used for the hangman character in *The Tragical Comedy or Comical Tragedy of Punch and Judy* by Giovanni Piccini and has become slang for an executioner.

The executioner's axe

THE DESTRUCTION
OF PORT ROYAL

England seized Jamaica in 1655 and the island became a vital base for privateers (ships licensed by the government) and fundamental to the English presence in the New World. The biggest settlement was Port Royal, built on a spit of land on the east of the island. It was full of taverns and bordellos frequented by pirates and an essential entrepôt for plundered goods and treasure. It soon became infamous as a den of depravity, known as the 'Sodom of the New World'.

On 7 June 1692, Port Royal was the epicentre of a massive earthquake. In the space of a couple of minutes the settlement was in ruins. Devastatingly, most of the city was built on sand, which liquefied in the quake. Houses sank rapidly into the sea and desperate people caught unawares were sucked down with their homes. When the trembling stopped, many remained buried and were suffocated. Survivors faced the secondary effects of starvation and disease. The eventual total death toll was around 3,000 (half of the population), and two-thirds of the city was destroyed. Many preachers in England believed the earthquake was a divine punishment for the wanton ways of the inhabitants. By the eighteenth century, after being struck by fires and hurricanes, Port Royal was largely abandoned. It is now a small fishing village.

THE LAST HABSBURG KING OF SPAIN

Philip IV of Spain died in 1665. His intended heir had been his first son, Baltasar Carlos, but he had died in 1646 after contracting smallpox. Left without a male heir, Philip decided to remarry. Rather unwisely, given his parents had been cousins, Philip's chosen bride was his niece, Mariana of Austria. They married in 1649 when he was forty-four and she fourteen.

After ten years of marriage Mariana had given birth to five children and only one, Margaret Theresa, had survived infancy. But in 1661 she produced a son, the future Charles II. Due to his inbreeding, Charles suffered from mental and physical disabilities and by the age of nine was unable to read or write. He had an over large tongue, which made him unintelligible. He often drooled, found it difficult to chew and suffered from gastric fever. He was bow-legged and unable to stand upright unless he leaned on something. The papal nuncio described him as torpid, indolent and stupefied, 'as weak in body as in mind'.

During his reign Charles was unable to attend any government meetings and deemed incapable of decision-making. He married twice but died childless in 1700. Disputes over his succession plunged Europe's major powers into war and Charles's final legacy was the War of the Spanish Succession, which lasted until 1714.

Enlightenment
and Revolution

c. AD 1700 to 1800

BROKEN ON THE WHEEL: THE LIFE
AND DEATH OF JOHANN PATKUL

W HEN JOHANN PATKUL was born in 1660 Sweden
ruled over an empire covering Finland, the Baltic States
and parts of Poland and Germany. Patkul's family were
nobles from Swedish-ruled Livonia, a region located in modern
Estonia and Latvia. Patkul served in the Swedish army and acted as
a representative of the Livonian gentry to air the grievances of the
region to the Swedish king, Charles XI. In 1694, Patkul expressed
himself too vehemently and was condemned to death for sedition.
He fled, unable to return to Swedish lands under pain of death.

Patkul began working as a diplomat for two of Sweden's rivals:
Augustus the Strong, King of Poland and Elector of Saxony, and Peter

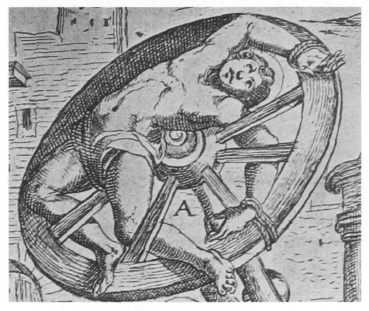

Breaking on the wheel

the Great of Russia. He helped create a Saxon-Polish-Russian-Danish coalition against Sweden, igniting the Great Northern War (1700–21). He hoped he would one day be able to return to his homeland.

But Patkul's fate was otherwise. When he failed to persuade Prussia to join the war against Sweden, Augustus had him imprisoned. Two years later, Charles XI made peace with Augustus and one of the terms was that Patkul must be returned to Sweden. As a traitor he was condemned to be broken on the wheel. When he had been tied to the spokes a sledgehammer was used to crush his arms and legs. He was then beheaded. In 1710, Russia won control of the Baltic lands, replacing Sweden as the dominant power in the region.

ISMAIL IBN SHARIF:
TYRANT KING OF MOROCCO

The Alaouite Dynasty had ruled Morocco since 1631. Their second king was Ismail Ibn Sharif, who seized power in 1672 after the death of his half-brother Al-Rashid. He was renowned for a lavish building programme in Meknes, the new capital. He roamed the building sites armed with a rifle, shooting anyone found slacking. Other slaves were repeatedly thrown into the air by their limbs until their necks were broken. His cruelty saw no limits when faced with rebels. In stamping out a revolt of Berbers in the south, his army collected the heads of 12,000 men, women and children to be displayed in the capital.

In the early eighteenth century, Ismail faced revolt from his son Mulai Muhammad, who was unhappy his half-brother Mulai Zidan had been designated heir. In 1705, Mulai Muhammad was captured and punished. One of his hands and one of his feet were sawn off and then plunged into hot pitch to cauterize them. He died soon after. This did not bring peace. By 1707, Ismail believed his heir Mulai Zidan had become too powerful, so bribed members of his harem to smother his son while he slept. Ismail ruled for another twenty years, facing near-constant revolts and family feuds. He died in 1727, igniting a bloody struggle for succession among his numerous sons.

PETER BECOMES 'GREAT'

Tsar Feodor III died in 1682 leaving Russia to his younger brothers, Peter I and Ivan V. Ivan was dull and sickly while Peter was bright and charismatic. Peter became sole ruling tsar in 1696 after the death of Ivan.

In 1697, Peter decided to tour Europe. The plan was unpopular and led to an abortive revolt. Peter had the rebel leaders killed and left their bodies to rot in Red Square. He spent eighteen months touring Germany, Austria, the Netherlands, and England, returning home in August 1698 to put down a revolt of the *streltsy* (an elite guards unit), executing some of the participants personally.

Peter's mission was to modernize Russia. One of his first acts was to hack off the traditional long beards of nobles and churchmen and insist on the wearing of western clothes. He also founded St Petersburg in 1703 and made it his capital in 1710. In foreign policy, he defeated Sweden and Poland-Lithuania to become the dominant power in the region. In 1721, he gave himself the new title 'Emperor of All Russia'. Peter had become 'Great'.

FAMILY PROBLEMS

Peter married Eudoxia Lopukhina in 1689 and she produced an heir, the tsarevich Alexei. However, Peter grew tired of his traditional Russian noble wife. They divorced and Eudoxia was sent to a convent. In 1707, Peter remarried. His new wife, Catherine, was a commoner from Latvia who had been servant to one of Peter's friends before catching the tsar's eye. Their marriage was happy even though, after eleven children, there was no surviving male.

As Peter carried out his reforms his relationship with Alexei became strained and in 1716 Alexei fled Russia. Two years later, Peter persuaded him to return, promising he would allow him to retire quietly. But Peter did no such thing. He forced his son to renounce his claim to the throne and had him cruelly interrogated and punished with the knout, a heavy scourge-like whip that inflicted horrific injuries. Peter convened a show trial to convict his son of treason and sentence him to death. Alexei, weakened by sickness and his injuries, died before he could be executed. His mother Eudoxia was hauled out of her convent, accused of debauchery, and sent to Lake Ladoga, near Finland. The abbess of the convent was knouted, and Eudoxia's suspected lover was accused of adultery and impaled.

By the 1720s, despite being the unchallenged master of the country, Peter's health was declining. He suffered from an inflamed urinary tract and acute bladder problems. His doctors diagnosed urinary retention and a catheter was used to draw out any blocked fluid, which was foul smelling and putrid. Peter died on 28 January 1725. With no living sons, he was succeeded by his wife Catherine.

NADER SHAH AND
THE PLUNDER OF DELHI

Nader was born to a common family in the north-east of the Persian Empire. The ruling Safavid Dynasty had lost control and inter-tribal warfare beset the empire. Amid the chaos, Nader rose to become an influential warlord. In 1732, Nader overthrew Shah Tadhmasp II, installing Tadhmasp's young son, Abbas III, on the throne. But Nader was the true power and, in 1736, he deposed Abbas and became shah.

In 1738, Nader successfully invaded Afghanistan. Advancing east, his target was the Mughal Empire, which ruled most of the Indian subcontinent. Its emperor, Muhammad Shah, struggled to control his subjects. On 24 February 1739, Nader routed the army Muhammad Shah had sent to stop at him at Karnal, 80 miles north

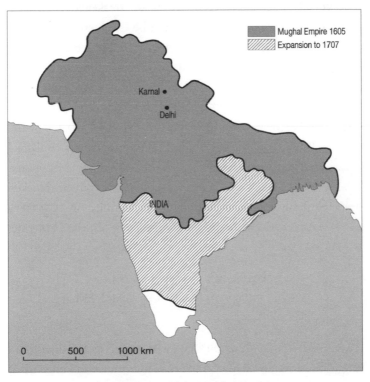

The expansion of the Mughal Empire

of Delhi. Muhammad Shah was captured, and agreed to let the Persians enter Delhi without opposition. They did so on 20 March.

At first, Nader commanded restraint from his soldiers, decreeing that any found to have injured a citizen would have their nose and ears cut off. But when a rumour spread that Nader had been killed the citizens of Delhi began attacking Persians, dispatching 900 soldiers. Nader ordered his men to retaliate: no one was to be left alive where his men had been harmed. The following morning around 20,000 were killed. Their bodies were left to rot in the streets.

Nader agreed to withdraw upon payment of a massive indemnity. Muhammad Shah gave him license to ransack his treasury, losing his lavish Peacock Throne and the famed Koh-i-Noor ('Mountain of Light') diamond (at the time the biggest in the world, and now part of the British crown jewels). The value of the plundered goods was around £100 billion in today's money. It took 30,000 camels and 24,000 mules to carry the treasure back to Persia.

NADER THE DESPOT

While Nader had been in India his son Reza Qoli Mirza had ruled Persia. Their relationship was strained as Nader became suspicious of overthrow. In 1741, a failed assassination attempt on Nader was (wrongly) blamed on Reza, and Nader had his son blinded. Nader quickly regretted his action and fell into a deep depression, becoming increasingly paranoid and tyrannical.

When a former ally of Nader's, Taqi Khan, revolted in 1744, Nader advanced on his stronghold at Shiraz (a city in south-eastern Iran) and brutally put down the rebellion. He executed thousands, and built two towers from their skulls. Taqi Khan was captured and castrated. He was blinded in one eye – the other was left so he could see his brother and sons being killed and his most beloved wife raped by Nader's soldiers.

In 1747, Nader's reign of terror came to an end when some of his officers, fearing that the increasingly capricious shah might put them to death, surprised him in his tent and cut off his head. Fifty years of civil war then beset Persia as numerous successors tried, and failed, to hold on to the throne.

CULLODEN: THE END OF THE JACOBITES

Queen Anne was the last Stuart monarch of Britain and Ireland. On her death in 1714, her closest living relative was her exiled half-brother James Francis Edward Stuart and, as a Catholic, he was barred from succeeding. The new king was Anne's nearest Protestant relative: a German prince, George of Hanover. James attempted to seize the throne but failed and died in exile in France. In 1745, James's son, Charles Edward Stuart, landed in Scotland to overthrow the Hanoverian king, George II, and restore a Stuart king to the throne. His followers were known as the Jacobites.

At first Charles's campaign was successful but once he crossed into England he found fewer followers. He retreated to the Highlands, the heartland of his support. Following him was an English army. They met on 16 April 1746 at Culloden, near Inverness. Despite an unfavourable strategic position, Charles refused to retreat and ordered an advance, into sleet. The Jacobites were met with a hail of artillery and were forced to retreat in disorder. English cavalry chased the stragglers, cutting them down as they attempted to flee. Wounded Jacobite soldiers were systematically murdered as they lay on the battlefield. Around 2,000 Jacobites died in battle.

The Jacobite cause was crushed. Charles managed to escape capture and returned to Europe. The Highland clans who had supported Charles faced repression and over the eighteenth century most were forced off their lands to make way for sheep farming.

CROWN PRINCE SADO

In 1749, King Yeongjo of Korea made his son Sado the crown prince and his heir designate. Sado's behaviour was violent and erratic. In 1757, he killed a eunuch – cutting off his head and brandishing it to an assembled crowd of courtiers. Sado developed a phobia of clothing. Every morning, twenty to thirty suits were laid out for him. Sado would burn some as an offering to ghosts, and then choose one to wear. If he found any small error in how they were laid out, Sado would injure or kill the servant responsible. He also insisted that the roads had to be completely cleared when he was travelling and if he saw anyone he would remove his clothes and burn them.

In 1761, Sado beat his secondary consort to death, and began to spend most of his time wandering the countryside incognito, throwing wild parties with travellers. He summoned fortune-tellers but they were killed if they made predictions he did not like. Sado's residence was funereal and he constructed himself a grave-sized subterranean chamber in which he would lie for hours. Eventually Yeongjo decided Sado's violent behaviour would imperil the royal family and he ordered the death of his son in 1762. The execution method could not be one for a common criminal, as this would taint the honour of the royal family. Sado was to be sealed in a rice chest. He died after eight days. Yeongjo passed away in 1776, and Sado's son Jeongjo became king.

THE LISBON EARTHQUAKE

At 9.40 a.m. on 1 November 1755, the strongest seismic event in recorded European history devastated Lisbon. The city was one of the wealthiest in Europe. However, its houses were built of stone and closely packed together in a maze of narrow streets. The tremors lasted between three and six minutes, opening fissures 5 metres wide in the ground. Forty minutes later a huge tsunami hit, destroying coastal parts of the city. To make matters worse, the shocks had overthrown cooking stoves, which caused numerous small fires. These, together with blazes started by looters, formed a vast conflagration that would last five days. The largest public hospital in Lisbon was consumed, killing hundreds of invalid patients. Once the flames had died down, 85 per cent of Lisbon was in ruins and around one in five of its population of 275,000 was dead.

The destruction was not limited to Lisbon. The damage extended to the Azores and other parts of Portugal, as well as France, Spain and Morocco. The royal palace in Lisbon was destroyed, along with its 70,000-volume library, archives, and numerous masterpieces, including works by Titian and Rubens. Fortunately, King Joseph I and the royal family had left Lisbon before the earthquake. Joseph later developed a fear of living within brick walls and moved his court to a complex of tents and pavilions on the outskirts of the city. Joseph's chief minister, the Marquess of Pombal managed the redevelopment of Lisbon almost single-handedly, overseeing the construction of a new, rational layout of wide streets and large squares with earthquake-resistant houses.

THE BLACK HOLE OF KOLKATA

The East India Company was founded in 1600. A joint-stock company trading with India, by the mid-eighteenth century it had also grown to become a powerful military force. One of its most important outposts was Fort William, in the Bengal city of Kolkata. The Indian ruler of Bengal, Nawab Siraj ud-Daulah was concerned with the Company's growing influence and power. In 1756, Siraj laid siege to the fort, whose commander was a Company bureaucrat, John Holwell. The fort was filled with hundreds of refugees from the nawab's armies but, due to desertions, there were only around 140 soldiers in the garrison. The fort fell on 20 June. Holwell claimed Siraj packed him and 145 others into a small cell in the fort known as the 'Black Hole'. It measured only 18 by 14 feet, and two small grilles in the wall provided the only ventilation. Those who fell to the ground were crushed in the darkness and the room was filled with the stench of sweat and human waste. The prisoners were left there for eleven hours. Holwell reported that only he and twenty-two others survived.

Subsequently, the veracity of Holwell's account has been questioned. It is likely that he exaggerated the numbers killed. The East India Company's response to the incident was swift. Robert Clive led their army against Siraj, overthrew him after the 1757 Battle of Plassey and then annexed Bengal. It was to be the beginning of British supremacy over India.

THE DEATH OF A REGICIDE

In January 1757, Robert-François Damiens, a mentally unstable servant, rushed at King Louis XV with a knife and stabbed him. It was the first attempt on a French king's life since the assassination of Henry IV in 1610. Louis' wounds were minor but Damiens was seized and sentenced to death by drawing and quartering. That March, the condemned man was carted to the Place de Grève, Paris's traditional place of public executions. Damiens was made to mount the scaffold and had the flesh torn from his torso, arm, thighs, and calves by red-hot pincers. His offending right hand, which had swung the knife against the king, was burned with sulphur. Into his wounds was poured a mixture of molten lead, boiling oil, burning resin, wax and sulphur. Damiens' arms and legs were then bound to four horses but, unaccustomed to the strain, the animals were unable to dismember him. Two more horses were harnessed to Damiens' thighs and the executioner helped speed the process by hacking at the limbs. Even still, Damiens apparently showed signs of life as he was being torn apart. While gathered spectators cheered, his remains were burned and the ashes thrown to the wind.

DARYA SALTYKOVA

In the eighteenth century, serfdom in Russia bound peasants to landowners to work for them in perpetuity. Serfs were not treated well. Most infamous for her cruelty was the noblewoman,

Darya Saltykova. In 1756, her husband died and she inherited 600 serfs. She treated them with savage barbarity, subjecting them to punishments and beatings and torturing them for largely imagined crimes. After seven years and the unexplained disappearance of 138 girls and women, Saltykova's neighbours began complaining about her behaviour. She was arrested and imprisoned and, after a lengthy trial, was found guilty of murdering thirty-eight serfs in 1768 (there was insufficient evidence to convict her for more deaths). As the death penalty had been abolished during the reforms of Empress Catherine the Great, Saltykova's fate was unclear. She was sentenced to spend one hour exposed to the public in a pillory in Moscow and was then imprisoned in a specially constructed underground cell in Ivanovsky Convent (in Moscow), where she was confined in total darkness until her death. Those who had carried out her brutal orders were flogged and exiled to Siberia. When Saltykova died in 1801, she had been imprisoned for so long her gaolers no longer remembered her crime. Serfdom was eventually abolished in Russia in 1861.

THE FALL OF AYUTTHAYA

Ayutthaya (located north of Bangkok) was the capital of the Kingdom of Siam that ruled over a territory covering most of present-day Thailand. Siam's main rival in the region was the Kingdom of Burma, with which they had warred since the sixteenth century. In 1766, two Burmese armies had advanced through Siam and joined outside the walls of Ayutthaya to besiege the city. As the siege wore on, famine and illness were rife. To make matters worse, a fire in early 1767 destroyed 10,000 houses. The Siamese king, Ekkathat, offered to surrender to the Burmese and become their vassal. They turned down his offer. Unconditional submission was their goal.

On 7 April, the Burmese breached the walls and took the city. Their victorious army ran riot. Anything flammable was put to the torch and anything valuable was stolen. Images of the Buddha were stripped of their gold coating. Thousands of prisoners were enslaved and taken back to Burma – so many that even privates in the Burmese army went home with four slaves. A once great city was reduced to rubble. When the Burmese armies returned home that November to protect their lands from a Chinese invasion, Ekkathat managed to flee the city. He died of starvation ten days later while hiding from the Burmese. Siam was in turmoil until Taksin, a provincial governor, emerged to become king in 1768. He reigned until 1782 and brought peace, order, and security to the kingdom.

ADOLF FREDERICK EATS HIMSELF TO DEATH

Adolf Frederick was crowned King of Sweden in 1751. His reign saw the nation's power wane and the influence of the monarchy decline at the expense of Parliament. Adolf Frederick died suddenly on 12 February 1771 after gorging himself on a massive meal including caviar, lobster, smoked fish, and champagne. For dessert he had consumed numerous servings of his favourite confectionary *semla*, a rich spiced bun filled with almond paste and topped with whipped cream. He was succeeded by his son, Gustav III, who restored much of the monarchy's power before being shot at the opera in 1792. He died of his wounds.

THE END OF CAPTAIN COOK

James Cook led a series of three groundbreaking voyages across the Pacific from 1768. His voyages saw the first European landings on Australia's east coast and the first recorded circumnavigation of New Zealand. In July 1776, Cook left England for the final time. There were two ships in the expedition: Cook's vessel the HMS *Resolution* and HMS *Discovery*, captained by Charles Clerke. Eighteen months later, the Hawaiian Islands were sighted. On 17 January 1779, Cook landed on Kealakekua Bay, on Hawai'i Island, the largest and easternmost of the archipelago. He and his men were the first Europeans to visit the islands.

After a month the two ships left to continue their exploration. However, the foremast of the *Resolution* split four days out of Kealakekua Bay and Cook was forced to return there to make repairs. Rapport with the locals there, at first cordial, soon deteriorated. There were reported thefts of iron chisels and tongs (irreplaceable this far from home) from the ships. On 14 February, Cook led an expedition of marines to take the local king hostage so the tools would be returned. The Hawaiians fought against this attempt and Cook retreated. He was pursued and, while attempting to climb aboard a boat, was struck on the head with a club and then stabbed in the neck with a dagger. Cook fell in the surf and his head was shattered by another blow from the club. Clerke took over command of the expedition and, although he died of tuberculosis in August, the two ships managed to return to England in October 1780.

The death of Captain Cook

THE BLOODIEST PLACE IN THE AMERICAN WAR OF INDEPENDENCE

In 1775, violence erupted between the armies of the thirteen American colonies and the British crown. The colonists had formed a Continental Congress to self-govern and established their own army under George Washington. On 4 July 1776, the Americans famously declared independence. But two months later the British captured New York City and it became the scene of the greatest atrocity of the war.

British commander William Howe had 5,000 American prisoners to house but one-quarter of New York had just been destroyed by fire. At first the prisoners were accommodated in churches, colleges and the old city hall. They were packed so tightly that they had to take turns to stand near a window to avoid suffocation. None were killed but many were tormented by being ridden to the gallows with nooses round their necks. As the war continued, more American prisoners were sent to New York. There was no room for them on land, so Howe decided to make use of the ships anchored in the East River. The prisoners were packed in the holds without regard for hygiene or safety. The ships leaked and the British completely neglected their prisoners, seldom giving them clean water or food. Starvation and disease were rife and so infested were the ships with vermin that rats would attack the weakest prisoners. When the Americans reconquered New York in 1783, 11,500 had died in the prison ships – more casualties than in any battle of the war.

THE WAXHAW MASSACRE

In May 1780, British general Lord Cornwallis learned that a regiment of 400 American infantry under Abraham Buford was retreating into North Carolina, so he sent a detachment of 270 cavalry to intercept them. In command was Banastre Tarleton. Tarleton urged his men on so quickly that many horses collapsed under their riders but they managed to overtake the Americans on 29 May at Waxhaw in South Carolina. Despite his men being exhausted, Tarleton ordered an immediate attack. Buford readied his own men to meet the attack with a volley of musket fire but the order came too late and the British charge overwhelmed them. Buford attempted to capitulate but the ensign preparing to raise the white flag was shot. Tarleton's men showed no mercy. A surgeon present at the battle wrote, 'the demand for quarters, seldom refused to a vanquished foe was at once found to be in vain.' British troops scoured the battlefield, plunging their bayonets into any Americans still living. Buford managed to escape with one hundred men. The phrase 'Tarleton's Quarter' was coined, meaning to take no prisoners.

THE CRAWFORD EXPEDITION

In 1781, the Americans and their French allies captured Yorktown from the British. It signalled the end of major military operations but violence continued in the Ohio Territory. On 7 March 1782, a group of Pennsylvania militiamen raided the village of Gnadenhutten, Ohio, which was inhabited by Christian Indians. They accused the Indians of raiding their territory. The next day ninety-six Indian men, women and children were bound up, stunned and killed by scalping. The militiamen looted the village and then burned it down, along with the bodies.

That May, William Crawford led an expedition of 480 men to Ohio to destroy the Indian towns along the Sandusky River. On 4 June, they met 300 Indians and Loyalists. Fighting continued over the next two days. Crawford was captured and the Indians, eager for revenge after Gnadenhutten, stripped and bound him. He was beaten and tied to a post with a long rope. Hot coals were laid around the post and Crawford was forced to walk barefoot over them, all the while being pelted with hot coals and gunpowder squibs and poked with burning sticks. Crawford was scalped and coals were poured over his head. He died soon after and his body was burned.

News of Crawford's death led to increased antipathy between Indians and settlers. The 1783 Treaty of Paris ended the war and the British officially recognized American independence, giving up control of Ohio and abandoning their erstwhile Indian allies. By 1795, after a decade of conflict, the Americans forced the Indians to turn over most of the territory.

THE FIRST FLEET

On 13 May 1787, a fleet of eleven ships left England to colonize Australia, commanded by Captain Arthur Phillip. There were just over 1,000 in the fleet, including 696 convicts. The British government planned to use Australia to cleanse the nation of its criminal class. Until now, convicts were imprisoned in decommissioned ships harboured on the Thames. Most were poor and desperate, and their crimes minor. One had been condemned to transportation for stealing two hens, another for thieving twelve cucumber plants, and another – an eleven-year-old boy – for stealing 10 yards of ribbon and a pair of silk stockings.

During the voyage the convicts lived in cramped, unsanitary conditions with no access to natural light. Due to a crooked contractor, their bread ration was limited to two slices per day. After an eight-month voyage of around 15,000 miles, they landed at the site that would become Sydney. The settlers, who had limited knowledge of farming, were expected to live off an unfamiliar land. Supplies ran low, starvation was rife and unruly convicts faced the lash. In spite of numerous difficulties the colonists, both convict and free, did survive and eventually prosper to forge a nation.

THE FRENCH REVOLUTION AND THE END OF THE MONARCHY

In the late 1780s, France was virtually bankrupt. In May 1789, King Louis XVI was forced to summon the Estates-General (an assembly of the nation's three estates: nobility, church, and commoners) to solve the financial problems. Royal power was unravelling. That July the Bastille was stormed and in October a mob invaded Versailles and forced Louis and the royal family to move to the Tuileries Palace in Paris. In 1791, Louis signed an agreement making France a constitutional monarchy. This arrangement did not last.

In August 1792, the Paris Commune, supported by the Jacobin political faction, dominated the capital, sparking a wave of violence.

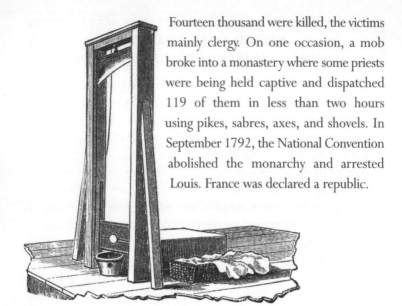

Fourteen thousand were killed, the victims mainly clergy. On one occasion, a mob broke into a monastery where some priests were being held captive and dispatched 119 of them in less than two hours using pikes, sabres, axes, and shovels. In September 1792, the National Convention abolished the monarchy and arrested Louis. France was declared a republic.

On trial, Louis was found guilty of conspiring 'against the public liberty' and sentenced to death. The method would be the guillotine.

The beheading device, introduced the previous year, would become the most enduring symbol of Revolutionary justice. The execution took place on 21 January 1793. Louis told the assembled crowd, 'I hope that the shedding of my blood will contribute to the happiness of France and you, unfortunate people...', before the blade silenced him. His unpopular Austrian wife, Marie-Antoinette, was executed that October. His son, who royalists declared Louis XVII, remained under arrest and died in June 1795 of scrofula, a form of tuberculosis.

KILLED IN THE BATH:
THE ASSASSINATION OF MARAT

In the turmoil that followed the execution of Louis XVI, the Jacobins seized control of the National Convention and the Committee of Public Safety, which would become the executive power of France. They were determined to maintain control of the Revolution, and set about rooting out any domestic opponents – particularly the more moderate Girondist faction. One of the most vocal supporters of the Jacobins and *sans-culottes* (the radical partisans of the lower classes) was the journalist Jean-Paul Marat. He had been a member of the National Convention but was forced to retire in June 1793 due to a chronic skin condition and a lung ailment. To relieve the pain of his illness he spent most of his time immersed in a special bathtub shaped like a shoe and fitted with a writing board. On 13 July, a young woman from Caen called Charlotte Corday, a Girondist sympathizer, sought an audience with Marat. She revealed she had a list of Girondists in her home town. 'Excellent!' declared Marat, writing down the names, 'In a few days time I shall have them all guillotined.' At that Corday unsheathed a knife concealed in her blouse. She plunged it into Marat's chest, slicing through his lung and aorta. Hearing the struggle, Marat's friends ran in. One of them broke a chair over Corday and restrained her. She was arrested and executed by the guillotine on 17 July, her body slung into a common trench.

MAXIMILIEN ROBESPIERRE AND THE TERROR

After Marat's assassination the Jacobin Maximilien Robespierre, a member of the Committee of Public Safety, rose to become the leading figure in France. In September 1793, he formally instituted the Reign of Terror to eliminate the Girondists and any other domestic enemies. The 'Law of Suspects' was passed, which created tribunals to seek out and execute any enemies of the Revolution. The list of offences defined as counter-revolutionary was so long that in a short period 250,000 people were imprisoned to await trial. Robespierre defended the Terror as 'nothing else than justice – prompt, severe, inflexible'.

One of Robespierre's most eager supporters was Jean-Baptiste Carrier, charged with eliminating Girondists and other counter-revolutionaries in Brittany. Carrier did not rely solely on the guillotine. He favoured mass executions, in which suspects were loaded onto barges that were then flooded, drowning all on board. Carrier called this 'vertical deportation'.

In June 1794, Robespierre passed a new law that abolished the normal rules of evidence, which allowed 'moral proofs' of guilt, and abolished the rights of the accused to make any defence. The violence escalated. Eventually there was a backlash against the increasingly arbitrary onslaught of the Terror. In July 1794, Robespierre was overthrown, arrested and executed. Forty thousand had been killed during his Reign of Terror.

In 1795, a new constitution was adopted. France would have two legislative houses and executive power fell on five 'directors'. This 'Directory' remained in place until 1799, when a general called Napoleon Bonaparte made himself the head of state.

Depiction of Robespierre's Reign of Terror

RUSSIA'S MOST DARING GENERAL: ALEXANDER SUVOROV

During the late eighteenth century, Alexander Suvorov rose to the rank of general in Russia's near-constant wars. One of his greatest victories was at Izmail, a strategically vital Ottoman settlement in modern-day Ukraine. Izmail had been under siege by the Russians since March 1790 and Suvorov was ordered to take control. His men stormed the town on 22 December and, under heavy fire, they scaled the defences. The combat was ferocious, but the Russians pushed on to victory. In the terrible struggle 26,000 Ottomans were killed, 1,000 of whom were bayoneted to death, despite having surrendered, when one of their number shot a Russian. The victorious army spent three days looting Izmail, after which so laden were they with Turkish clothing they were barely recognizable as Russian soldiers.

MASSACRE OF PRAGA

By the 1790s, Russia had annexed half of Poland-Lithuania. In 1794, the Polish general Tadeusz Kosciuszko led an uprising. He was captured in October, leaving Suvorov free to advance on Warsaw. The only thing standing in his way was the suburb of Praga, divided from Warsaw by the Vistula River. Suvorov launched an all-out surprise attack on Praga on 4 November. Many Poles tried to flee across the Vistula but the Russians burned the bridges, trapping thousands. Many drowned attempting to swim to safety. When civilians starting throwing missiles at the Russians, Suvorov ordered his men to massacre any that stood against them. Polish soldiers and civilians were cut down by Russian artillery. In total, 13,000 Polish soldiers and 7,000 civilians were killed. The Russians now dominated Poland, which lost its independence for over a century. Suvorov died in 1800. In nearly twenty-five years as a general, he never lost a battle.

Empire

c. AD 1800 to 1880

THE MAD KING OF BRITAIN

GEORGE III ASCENDED to the British throne in 1760. In the latter part of his reign he suffered from bouts of melancholy, which gave way to insanity. The first spell came in 1788, when George suffered from a 'pretty smart bilious attack'. He was treated in his residence at Kew where physicians gave him strong laxatives and laudanum (a potent tincture containing opium). Irritating poultices were spread over George's body to bring up blisters, which it was believed would draw out the 'evil humours' that caused his madness. The treatments failed to improve the king's behaviour, which became increasingly erratic. His speech was slurred and he suffered from severe delusions: believing London had been flooded, that he could see Hanover in a telescope, and that an oak tree he saw when out walking in Windsor Park was the King of

Prussia (George was reported to have shaken one of its branches like a hand and spent some time talking to it). The king was forced to wear a straightjacket, and was even bound to an iron chair. Parliament began to ask whether George's son the Prince of Wales ought to stand in as regent, but then the king rallied and recovered his health. George suffered from a relapse in 1801 and ten years later was sent to live out his days at Windsor Palace. In his final years he became increasingly deaf and blind and was unable to recognize his own wife. He died on 29 January 1820. The Prince of Wales, who had been sworn in as regent in 1811, succeeded his father as George IV.

'THE PRINCE OF WHALES'
BECOMES KING

The younger George was described by *The Times* as a man whose only states of happiness were 'gluttony, drunkenness, and gambling'. He was a notorious philanderer and at the age of sixteen seduced one of the queen's maids of honour. In 1785, he secretly (and illegally) married the twice-widowed Catholic Maria Fitzherbert without the permission of the king.

In 1795, George was legally married to the German princess Caroline of Brunswick. The two eventually came to hate each other so much that George barred Caroline from his coronation. Once king, George IV became obese. According to the Duke of Wellington, a typical breakfast would be a portion of pie containing two pigeons and three beef steaks, along with wine, champagne, port and brandy – all followed with a dose of laudanum. He suffered from gout and an inflamed bladder. Ensconced in his lavish new palace in Brighton, George treated his maladies by opening his veins to bleed himself. He wore corsets to control his sizeable girth and applied numerous creams and ointments to make him appear younger. George IV died in 1830. His only legitimate child, Princess Charlotte Augusta, had died in 1817, so his brother succeeded him as William IV.

MURDER ON THE FRONTIER: THE HARPE BROTHERS

The Harpe Brothers were infamous in their native North Carolina and soon built up an unsavoury reputation in Tennessee. Accused of unsolved murders and with the theft of hogs and sheep, Micajah ('Big Harpe') and Willey ('Little Harpe') were imprisoned with the three women they lived with – two of whom were pregnant. In March 1798, the Harpe Brothers escaped and fled north towards Kentucky. The Harpe women and their newborn children were released and rejoined their men, but the squalling infants so irritated Micajah that he dashed one of them against a tree. The Harpes set about a spree of violence across southern Illinois, Kentucky, and Tennessee, wantonly murdering dozens of men, women, and children. The governor of Kentucky offered a reward for anyone who found them. In July 1799, a mob led by Moses Stegall, whose wife and baby had been murdered by the brothers, tracked down Micajah in Kentucky. Micajah was shot in the side and Stegall cut off his head while he was still conscious. Micajah's body was left to rot and his head was displayed on a tree at a nearby crossroads. Willey escaped capture but was eventually tracked down in Mississippi in 1803. He was formally tried for his crimes and hanged in 1804.

THE ASSASSINATION OF EMPEROR PAUL I OF RUSSIA

Emperor Paul I was the son of Catherine the Great and the great-grandson of Peter the Great. He succeeded Catherine in 1796 and was determined to liberalize Russia, reversing many of his mother's severe policies. Paul's ambitious reforms quickly alienated many officers of the Russian military, who conspired to overthrow the emperor. Paul, paranoid about the plots against him, had recently moved into a new residence in St Petersburg. St Michael's Castle was protected by drawbridges and waterways. Even so, on the night of 23 March 1801, a group of plotters infiltrated the castle and broke into Paul's bedroom. The emperor had no time to flee so hid behind a screen. The plotters felt that Paul's bed was still warm and, when the moon broke from behind a cloud, they caught sight of him in his hiding place. They dragged him to his desk and ordered he sign an order of abdication. Paul resisted and a struggle broke out, in which the emperor was struck by a sword and his head was slammed against a marble-topped table. He was then trampled on and strangled to death with a guardsman's sash. Paul's son Alexander was proclaimed emperor and ruled until 1825.

TOUSSAINT LOUVERTURE
AND THE BLOODY STRUGGLE FOR
FREEDOM IN HAITI

The Caribbean island of Hispaniola (modern Haiti and the Dominican Republic) was colonized by France and Spain. The year 1791 saw a slave revolt against the French with Toussaint Louverture as its figurehead. Allied with Spain, Toussaint's ragged army defied the French. In 1794, the French revolutionary government abolished slavery. Toussaint switched his allegiance to France, helping them force out Spain.

In 1801, Toussaint made himself lifelong governor-general of the island. By this time Napoleon Bonaparte had won control of France. Alarmed at Toussaint's growing authority, he sent his brother-in-law Charles Emmanuel Leclerc to Hispaniola to re-establish slavery and make the colony plantations more profitable. Toussaint was captured in 1802 and shipped to France. He was denied medical attention and died on 7 April 1803 in his cold, damp cell.

Toussaint's chief lieutenant, Jean-Jacques Dessalines, assumed leadership of the struggle against the French. Leclerc had died in 1802 and the new French leader, Donatien Rochambeau, was a savage man who considered blacks inferior to animals. He imported 1,500 wild dogs from Cuba to track down the black inhabitants. Some prisoners were tied to posts, their bellies cut open so that Rochambeau's dogs could devour their intestines. Others were buried up to their necks near insect colonies and left to die. The black population fell from 500,000 in 1791 to just 350,000. Yet Dessalines and his army fought on while yellow fever began to decimate the

French. Eventually Rochambeau agreed to evacuate on 19 November 1803 and Dessalines became leader of an independent, free island.

In 1804, Dessalines ordered a massacre of all non-blacks, sparing only a few priests and professionals. He instituted a system of forced labour, where all people except soldiers were attached to plantations. He became unpopular and was assassinated in 1806.

1812: THE BEGINNING OF NAPOLEON'S DOWNFALL

Napoleon Bonaparte rose to prominence during the French Revolution. He seized power in 1799 and in 1804 he was proclaimed Emperor of France. Under his leadership France became the dominant power in Europe, with Napoleon defeating all who opposed him. But in 1812 the tide began to turn.

THE SIEGE OF BADAJOZ

In 1807, Napoleon allied with Spain against Portugal. But the following year he turned on the Spanish and installed his brother Joseph as King of Spain. The Spanish embarked on a savage guerrilla war against the occupying French. A British army landed in Portugal under Sir Arthur Wellesley, who would later be awarded the title Duke of Wellington. In 1812, Wellesley led an Anglo-Portuguese force of 27,000 into Spain with the aim of driving out the French. Their first major target was the border town of Badajoz. On 16 March, the siege began. The French held against forty assaults in twenty-one days but on 6 April the defences were breached. Wellesley had lost 4,800 men. His victorious army ravaged the town, killing 4,000 civilians. A private recalled, 'there was not … a house in the whole town that was not ransacked … murder, rape, and robbery were committed with the greatest impunity.' The streets were filled with thousands of drunken soldiers. Order was not restored until 9 April. By 1814, the French had been driven out of Spain.

THE RETREAT FROM MOSCOW

In June 1812, Napoleon led an army of around half a million into Russia, winning an early victory at Smolensk. Subsequently the Russian army retreated, forcing Napoleon to advance into the interior. The Russians adopted a scorched-earth policy, destroying anything of use to the invaders. On 7 September, the two armies clashed at Borodino, west of Moscow, in what was the bloodiest clash in military history until the Battle of the Somme. Napoleon was victorious but lost 28,000 men. The Russians lost 45,000. Napoleon entered Moscow, only to find a city devastated by fires set by the Russians. With his supply lines stretched and the Russians defiant, Napoleon decided to retreat in mid-October.

With few horses progress was slow and in November the Russian winter began to set in. The soldiers had no warm clothes, and were forced to improvise with women's dresses and clerical vestments. Food supplies dwindled, so the men turned to horse and cat flesh, or biscuits made from water and chopped-up straw. Tallow candles were stirred into porridge to add fat. Frostbite and diarrhoea were endemic. Cossack cavalry constantly harried the retreating columns, finding amusement in making off with men and stripping them naked to die in the snow.

Return of the French army from Moscow

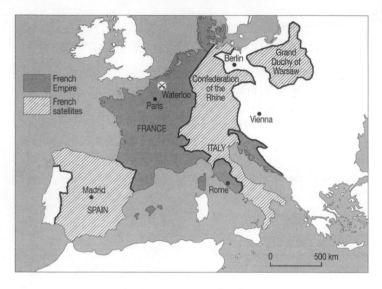

French
Empire

French
satellites

Berlin

Grand
Duchy of
Warsaw

Confederation
of the
Rhine

Waterloo

Paris

Vienna

FRANCE

ITALY

Madrid

Rome

SPAIN

0   500 km

Napoleon's empire at its height (1812)

In December, Napoleon's army exited Russian territory. Only 120,000 had survived the invasion. Napoleon was no longer invincible. His allies defeated him in 1814 and he was exiled to the Mediterranean island of Elba. Napoleon escaped and returned to power in 1815, before his final defeat at Waterloo. He was exiled again – this time to the remote Atlantic island of St Helena, where he died in 1821.

THE ERUPTION OF MOUNT TAMBORA

On 5 April 1815, Mount Tambora violently erupted. The sound was heard nearly 1,000 miles away from its location on Sumbawa Island in Indonesia. The eruption sent out 25 cubic miles of debris in a plume over 4,000 feet high. Savage whirlwinds swept across the island, throwing horses and cattle into the air and tearing up trees. Only twenty-six out of Sumbawa's population of 12,000 survived in the most explosive eruption in recorded history. The plume of ash was so large that some scientists believe it led to global cooling, which was particularly pronounced in Western Europe and North America and caused harvest failure and famine.

THE PETERLOO MASSACRE

After the Napoleonic Wars, Britain entered a recession. There was pressure to reform the electoral system, which disenfranchised millions – particularly in the north-west. In 1819, a mass meeting to demand reform was organized on St Peter's Field in Manchester. On 16 August, a crowd of around 80,000 gathered. Fearing a crisis, the authorities decided to put a stop to the meeting and constables were ordered in. Messages were sent to two cavalry regiments asking for help. Once the constables and cavalry converged on the field, chaos ensued. As people fled the soldiers lost discipline, swiping indiscriminately with their sabres. In the melee, around 500 were wounded and fifteen died. The public were horrified at the brutality. The event became known as 'Peterloo'. It was not until 1928 that all adults in Britain were given the vote.

DEATH BY WHALEBONE

Gouverneur Morris was a Founding Father of the United States, and one of the authors and signatories of the Constitution. Despite losing his leg in a 1780 carriage accident (it was replaced with a wooden peg leg), Morris was an influential political force. He also found time for numerous affairs, finally marrying in 1809 at the age of fifty-seven. Morris had prostate cancer and suffered from gout, which caused a painful blockage of his urinary tract. To relieve the pain, Morris attempted self-surgery by inserting a whalebone into his urethra. This only exacerbated his illness and Morris died shortly afterwards.

VAN DIEMEN'S LAND

In 1803, the British colonized Van Diemen's Land (known as Tasmania after 1856). Until the abolition of penal transportation in 1853, the colony was the primary destination for convicts sent to Australia. Most worked as labourers or servants for free settlers. The worst offenders were sent to labour in harsh conditions at the penal settlement of Macquarie Harbour, which was located on Sarah Island, off the west coast of Van Diemen's Land.

ALEXANDER PEARCE

Few convicts escaped Macquarie Harbour, but one man did it twice. Alexander Pearce was an Irishman who had been transported in 1819 for stealing six pairs of shoes. Pearce arrived in Van Diemen's

Land in 1820 and worked as a servant. He ran into trouble for drunkenness, stealing and absconding. In 1822, he was sent to Macquarie Harbour.

That September Pearce and seven other convicts stole a boat and rowed to the mainland. They planned to hike east across Van Diemen's Land to Hobart and then escape to England. Food ran out after a week. After four days without provisions, one of the convicts, Robert Greenhill, slew another with an axe. The group ate his remains. Two of the party, fearing they might be next, turned back to Macquarie Harbour. They were found half-dead on 12 October and both died soon after..

Two more men were killed and eaten that month. Now only Greenhill and Pearce remained. Pearce, convinced that Greenhill planned to kill him, murdered the other man while he slept. After eight weeks on the run, Pearce met a shepherd. He was also Irish and introduced Pearce to a couple of bandits, who sheltered him. The authorities caught up with Pearce on 11 January 1823. He confessed to cannibalism but the story was dismissed as fantastical. Pearce was returned to Macquarie Harbour.

On 16 November, Pearce escaped with another convict, Thomas Cox. Pearce was found after five days and confessed to having eaten Cox two days earlier. He showed his captors Cox's body. It had been sliced through the middle with the head and privates removed, and flesh had been cut from the calves, thighs, loin and arms – which Pearce told them was 'the most delicious food'. Pearce was shipped to Hobart and hanged on 19 July 1824.

EXTERMINATION OF THE ABORIGINES

When the British settled in Van Diemen's Land, 4,000 Aborigines lived there. They had little or no legal protection from white settlers and there were rumours that kangaroo hunters shot them to feed their dogs. In the 1820s, a boom in wool prices led to an increase in sheep farming, bringing more white settlers. In 1828, the Lieutenant-Governor of Van Diemen's Land, George Arthur, declared martial law, effectively making it legal for settlers to shoot Aborigines on sight. In 1830, Arthur offered a bounty of £5 for the capture of adult Aborigines and £2 for children with the aim of forcibly relocating them to unsettled areas. These laws, coupled with European diseases, would eventually wipe out the Tasmanian Aborigines. In 1876, the last full-blooded Tasmanian Aborigine, Trugernanner, died. Her corpse was exhumed and boiled and her skeleton was then put on public display, where it remained until 1947.

THE CHIOS MASSACRE

From the fifteenth century, the Ottoman Empire ruled most of Greece. In the early nineteenth century, the Greeks struggled against Turkish rule and armed revolt began in 1821. The Aegean island of Chios was one of the wealthiest parts of Greece. On 22 March 1822, rebels from the nearby island of Samos landed on Chios to support the rebellion. The rebels were successful at first, but when reinforcements arrived in the form of a Turkish fleet, most of the Samians fled. The Turks regained Chios and were determined to enforce their authority. One of their first actions was to assail a monastery where the clergy had taken refuge. The monastery was burned and the priests either died in the fire or were put to the sword. On 6 May, almost all of the Greek nobles on Chios were hanged – their bodies dangling lifeless from the trees around the main town square. The next month the Greek rebels sent two fire ships into the Turkish fleet, destroying their flagship. The islanders were left to face the vengeance of the Turks. Most of the villages on Chios were fired and the people were killed, imprisoned or exiled. Before the massacre, Chios's population was 120,000 but by the end of 1821 it had fallen to 30,000. Reports of the massacres caused outrage in Europe. It made the rebels more determined to win independence, which they achieved in 1832.

SHAKA ZULU'S LAST YEAR

In the early nineteenth century, the Zulu Kingdom became the most powerful in southern Africa. Their greatest ruler was Shaka Zulu, whose military reforms and leadership made his army one of the most formidable in the world. Shaka became king in 1816 and swiftly defeated his neighbouring tribes, subsuming them into his kingdom.

On 10 October 1827, Shaka's beloved mother Nandi died of dysentery. Shaka was distraught, killing forty oxen in mourning, and ordering 12,000 men to guard Nandi's grave for a year. Six women, whom he believed responsible for his mother's death, were executed by having thatching grass tied to them, which was then set alight. They were then forced to run until they collapsed and had their skulls crushed where they lay. To commemorate his mother, Shaka ordered a one-year period of mourning in which no cultivation could take place. The fields were not to be tended and the cow's milk was to be poured onto the ground. Sex was forbidden and women found to have become pregnant after the edict were to be put to death along with their husbands.

Shaka was consumed with melancholy and showed little interest in ruling his kingdom. On 7 September 1828, he declared the period of mourning to be over but it had seriously damaged his popularity. On 22 September, two of Shaka's half-brothers, Dingane and Mhlangana, attacked him with their spears. Shaka's chamberlain finished the job by stabbing him in the back. One of the greatest rulers in African history was buried in an unmarked grave.

QUEEN RANAVALONA OF MADAGASCAR

The Kingdom of Madagascar, an island off the east coast of Africa, was fiercely independent in the face of European colonial expansion. In 1828, King Radama I died. Ranavalona, one of his twelve senior wives, moved to seize the throne and was proclaimed queen on 1 August, having killed her chief rivals. With her position secure, Ranavalona used bloody methods to impose her will on Madagascar. Christian missionaries were expelled and Ranavalona made it a capital offence for her subjects to practise Christianity. Torture, crucifixion and beheadings were commonplace. Brigands, runaway slaves and rebels were flayed alive, sawn in half or had their testicles slowly crushed. Others were bound in buffalo hides with their heads protruding and left to die in the sun. The worst offenders were fastened to wooden stakes in waist-high pits, into which boiling water was poured.

TESTING FOR TREASON

Ranavalona became suspicious of potential traitors and developed a method for testing their guilt. The victim was given a meal of rice, three pieces of chicken skin and the seeds of a poisonous plant called *tanguena*. They were then forced to drink draughts of water until they vomited. If the three pieces of skin were disgorged, they were deemed innocent and released. If two or fewer came up, they were considered guilty and hauled away to be tortured and executed. Another test was progressive amputation. The victims' fingers, hands, feet, and limbs were cut off. After each amputation, the victim was invited to confess to their crimes. Ultimately no one could survive the ordeal, dying of shock or loss of blood if they did not confess.

Ranavalona died in her sleep in 1861, having reigned for thirty-three years. During her bloody rule the population of Madagascar had fallen by one-third. Despite this, Ranavalona had maintained Madagascar's independence in the face of British and French incursions. Her son succeeded her as Radama II and opened the island to Christianity and European traders. In 1863, his wife Rasoherina led a coup against him and he was deposed and strangled. She died in 1868 and was succeeded by another of Radama II's wives, Ranavalona II. Under this reign the royal family and court adopted Christianity and in 1896 France annexed Madagascar, ending the island's independence.

THE TRAIL OF TEARS

In 1830, President Andrew Jackson signed the Indian Removal Act, which led to the relocation of thousands of Native Americans from their homes in the south-eastern United States west to territory in Oklahoma. The process became known as the 'Trail of Tears'. The last of the tribal groups to be forced out was the Cherokee Nation. In 1836, they were given two years to leave Georgia. Twenty thousand Cherokee were removed from their homes at gunpoint, and forced into 'containment camps', which were little more than unhygienic, fenced-off pens. Once they had been evicted, the Cherokee were forced to march to Oklahoma. Eight thousand died in the horrific process.

THE MALÊ REVOLT

From the sixteenth to the nineteenth centuries, 4 million Africans were enslaved and transported to Brazil, mostly to work on sugar plantations. The state of Bahia, on the Atlantic coast, was a major centre of sugar production and had a high population of slaves. In 1835 a slave rebellion broke out in Bahia's capital, Salvador, inspired by Muslim (known as 'malê') leaders. The uprising was swiftly put down and retribution was harsh. Innocent blacks were killed and beaten in the streets – the chief of police recorded that 'murders without motive go on in public'. Rebels were flogged, imprisoned, sentenced to forced labour or deported to Africa. Four of the ringleaders were sentenced to death, and killed by firing squad.

THE RETREAT FROM KABUL

In 1838, the East India Company sent an army into Afghanistan to overthrow its ruler, the emir Dost Mohammad Khan, who was considered too Russian-friendly. A new emir, Shuja Shah Durrani, was installed and a garrison was placed in Kabul. Unrest followed.

In 1841, Dost Mohammad's son, Akbar Khan, emerged as the leader of a revolt. The British commander in Kabul, General William Elphinstone, was sickly and incompetent and failed to react effectively. Afghan mobs attacked his garrison and by winter its 4,500 soldiers and 12,000 relatives and camp followers were besieged in their cantonments outside the city. With supplies running low, a Company civil servant called William Macnaghten rode out to Kabul to negotiate surrender with Akbar Khan. Macnaghten was dragged away and killed. His head and limbs were paraded through the streets, and his torso was hung from a meat hook in the bazaar.

Elphinstone failed to exact any retribution. On New Years' Day 1842, he capitulated to the rebels and agreed to return to India. Elphinstone's army left Kabul on 6 January. Troops were reduced to a meagre daily ration of a handful of flour mixed with some melted butter. Exhausted, many camp followers simply sat by the road waiting to die.

On 11 January, the Afghans seized Elphinstone, who died in captivity. His army was unable to defend against constant Afghan attacks on their column and their numbers steadily dwindled. Almost none of the 16,500 survived to return to India. The British made no serious attempts to extend their rule over Afghanistan. In April 1842, Dost Mohammad returned to power, reigning until 1863.

THE IRISH POTATO FAMINE

The potato was a staple food in Ireland in the early nineteenth century. The average adult male worker ate around 12 pounds of potato per day and, combined with milk, the diet provided adequate sustenance. But this reliance on a single foodstuff would have fatal consequences.

In the 1840s, a fungal disease called *Phytopthora infestans*, or the potato blight, struck Europe. When it hit Ireland in 1845, it led to the partial failure of the potato harvest and in 1846 the harvest failed completely. Food prices rocketed and thousands died of starvation. Many could no longer afford to pay rent and were evicted from their land, leaving them with no way to make a living. The emaciated populace were prone to disease, with typhus, fever, dysentery and diarrhoea the biggest killers. One million people died of starvation and disease between 1846 and 1851.

THE IRISH DIASPORA

Around 1.5 million people emigrated from Ireland to the United States in the decade that followed the famine. The passage across the Atlantic took six to seven weeks and the vessels, which became known as 'coffin ships', were overcrowded and unhygienic. Over 50,000 migrants died during the crossing. In the aftermath of the famine years, Ireland's population virtually halved from 8.5 million in 1845 to just 4.5 million in the 1890s. Even by the twenty-first century, it has still not exceeded pre-famine levels.

CRIMEA

In 1853, France, Britain, Sardinia and the Ottoman Empire went to war with Russia. Most of the fighting took place in Russian-controlled Crimea, a peninsula on the Black Sea. In September 1854, an allied force landed in Crimea while the Russians regrouped to the fortified port of Sevastopol. As winter set in, the besieging army froze. The British soldiers were in their summer uniforms and their tents provided little protection. The officers were better sheltered than their men – some even wintered in Istanbul. The Earl of Cardigan, who had led the disastrous Charge of the Light Brigade, slept on board his private yacht.

British medical care was woeful. Over the winter, 4,000 British men died at their main barracks despite the best efforts of Florence Nightingale. Diseases, especially cholera, were responsible for more deaths than Russian attacks. The main British hospital was filthy and built on a cesspool. Sewers contaminated the drinking water. In the aftermath of Crimea and in the face of public outrage, the British army wholly reformed its outdated medical practices.

THE TAKING OF SEVASTOPOL

The besieged Russians in Sevastopol faced near-constant artillery bombardment, but the city's fortifications were strong. In September 1855, however, the French made a crucial breakthrough in the south of the city, and shortly afterwards the allies entered. A French source recalls that Sevastopol was 'literally crushed to bits'. The loss of the city proved disastrous for the Russians. They were forced to make peace early in 1856 at great cost to their prestige and influence.

THE LATTER DAY SAINTS

In 1823, Joseph Smith, Jr. received angelic visions inspiring him to write a new biblical testament, the Book of Mormon. He founded a new religion – the Church of Jesus Christ of Latter Day Saints. In 1831, the Saints settled in Ohio. They faced violent persecution and Smith and other Mormons were frequently tarred and feathered by hostile locals. Driven out in 1839, they relocated to Illinois, where they were similarly unpopular. In 1844, Smith was accused of destroying the printing press of a critical newspaper and imprisoned. On 27 June, a mob stormed Smith's cell. He was shot attempting to escape from a window. The main body of the Church migrated west and settled in Utah.

THE KING OF BEAVER ISLAND

In the aftermath of Smith's death, many of his followers splintered off and founded their own churches. One of them was James Strang, who established a settlement for his followers on Beaver Island on Lake Michigan in 1848. In 1850, Strang crowned himself 'king' of his church, and claimed authority over the entire island. He became increasingly dictatorial and began practising polygamy. In 1856, two of his disgruntled followers, Thomas Bedford and Alexander Wentworth, fired on Strang, hitting him in the head and in the small of his back. Wentworth then fired point-blank at Strang's head and Bedford clubbed him with the butt of his pistol until it broke. The killers fled to the mainland. Despite numerous witnesses, their crime went unpunished. Strang died of his wounds four weeks after the attack and his church withered away.

HOW A NEW CARTRIDGE DESIGN IGNITED THE INDIAN REBELLION

In 1857, the British East India Company ruled most of India (including modern Pakistan and Bangladesh). They had an army of 250,000 (80 per cent of whom were Indian recruits called 'sepoys'). As the Company expanded their rule, historic laws and traditions were eroded. Disquiet spread among the sepoys and Indian civilians.

The trigger for rebellion came in the form of a new gun cartridge. Rifle ammunition was pre-packed in greased paper cartridges that had to be bitten open. Rumours spread that the grease on these cartridges was made from beef and pork fat, which was deeply offensive to the sepoys, who were mostly Hindu or Muslim. On 29 March, an aggrieved sepoy called Mangal Pandey shot at a British officer. Pandey was captured and hanged and, to set an example, his entire regiment was disbanded.

Violence then erupted in April when the sepoys revolted in Meerut, North India, killing many of their officers. They then marched to Delhi, the only remnant of the Mughal Empire that had once ruled over all India. There, Emperor Bahadur Shah II gave his support to the rebels and violent opposition to the Company swiftly spread across India, among both sepoys and local rulers.

THE TWO MASSACRES OF CAWNPORE

In June 1857, rebels besieged the northern Indian town of Cawnpore (now Kanpur). The British had dug a trench to defend the town and were able to weather several attacks. But, after a few weeks, food was running out and the situation was hopeless for the British soldiers and their families in Cawnpore. The British surrendered. They were granted safe passage to retreat to Allahabad via boat, along the River Ganges.

On 27 June, the British prepared to leave Cawnpore but, as they loaded and boarded their boats at the river, the rebels attacked. One hundred and ninety-seven surviving women and children were led back to town and held hostage in a villa called the Bibighar. On 15 July, with the British on the verge of recapturing Cawnpore, the hostages were massacred and dismembered. Their bodies were thrown into a well. Only a handful of the 1,200 British soldiers and civilians had survived the two massacres.

BRITISH RETRIBUTION

When the British army entered Cawnpore and saw the effects of the massacre, their revenge was harsh and instant. Rebels were humiliated by being forced to eat beef or pork, or lick the bloody floor of the Bibighar. The British had earlier passed Act XIV, which empowered them to execute any Indian even suspected of rebellion and made sedition a capital offence. Roving bands of British volunteers roamed the countryside, stringing up suspected rebels from roadside gibbets – many of whom were innocent civilians who had not taken part in the rebellion. Other suspected rebels were bound across the mouth of a cannon, which was then fired. By 1859, the British had defeated the last of the rebels and on 8 July a state of peace was declared. In the aftermath of the rebellion, control of India passed from the East India Company to the Crown. The British Raj ruled until 1947.

THE CANING OF CHARLES SUMNER

In the mid-nineteenth century, the issue of slavery divided the United States. In the South slavery was fundamental to the economy but most in the North favoured abolition. In 1856, Charles Sumner, a Massachusetts senator, made a speech attacking slavery. Two days later, Preston Brooks, a South Carolina congressman, approached Sumner on the senate floor. Brooks beat Sumner over the head with his cane repeatedly, continuing even after he lost consciousness. Sumner was seriously injured and only returned to political life in 1859, after three years' medical treatment. Brooks escaped criminal

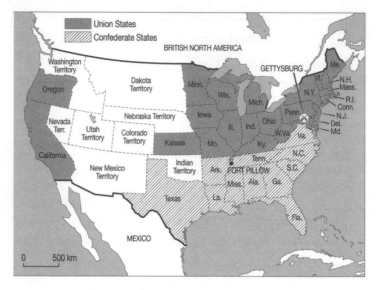

Division of territories in the US Civil War

charges and the incident further polarized the division between North and South. In March 1861, Abraham Lincoln was sworn in as President. In response, eleven Southern states seceded, forming the Confederate States of America and igniting a bloody four-year war.

THE FORT PILLOW MASSACRE

The fulcrum of the American Civil War was the Battle of Gettysburg (Pennsylvania), where the Union army defeated the Confederates in a three-day struggle that cost nearly 8,000 lives. Thereafter, the Union struck south, steadily defeating the Confederates.

In the midst of their eventual defeat, the Confederates were still determined fighters. In 1864, Confederate forces raided Kentucky

'BLOODY BILL' ANDERSON

While the Union and Confederate armies fought, a savage guerrilla conflict emerged in the Kansas–Missouri borderlands. Raiders from both sides attacked enemy territory. In 1863, Confederate guerrillas stormed the town of Lawrence, Kansas, burning houses. They spared women and children but killed all the men they saw. The most furious was William 'Bloody Bill' Anderson. He shot fourteen men, first making them crawl at his feet. Anderson then started his own band. He was notorious for vicious attacks on Union soldiers and sympathizers, killing them and scalping and mutilating their corpses. In 1864, Union forces killed Anderson near Albany, Missouri. On his person was a silk cord that he used to tally his kills – it had fifty-three knots.

and Tennessee. After a victory at Paducah, Kentucky, a detachment of 1,500 attacked Union-controlled Fort Pillow, Tennessee, on 12 April. It had a garrison of 557, about half of whom were black. Substantially outnumbered, the Union troops threw down their arms and surrendered. The Confederates then killed 300 unarmed and defenceless men in cold blood, with the black soldiers the main targets of violence. A Union officer was nailed to a burning building and left to die. Even one of the Confederate soldiers described the massacre as 'the most horrible sight that I have ever witnessed'.

The massacre became a byword for Confederate atrocity, and the Union army pressed on to finish the war. On 9 April 1865, the commander of the main Confederate army, Robert E. Lee, surrendered. Although there was some sporadic fighting in the weeks after this, it signalled the end of the Civil War, victory for the Union and the end of slavery in the United States. Sadly the architect of this victory, President Abraham Lincoln, did not live to guide the reconstruction of the nation. While attending the theatre six days later, he was shot and fatally wounded.

HONG XIUQUAN AND THE TAIPING REBELLION

The Taiping Rebellion was fought in China between 1850 and 1864 and cost at least 20 million lives, making it the bloodiest civil war in history.

The Taiping leader was Hong Xiuquan. As a young man, he had failed the examination to join the civil service and had fallen into a trance. On his recovery, he announced he had seen visions of God and Heaven. He set out to crusade against idol-worship and overthrow China's ruling Qing Dynasty. Hong, claiming to be God's son and Jesus's brother, founded a religion partly based on Christianity. It attracted thousands of followers in the Guangxi region of Southern China.

In 1850, Hong's army defeated imperial forces sent to destroy them. They then marched against the Qing, winning a series of victories. In 1853, they captured Nanjing. Hong made it the capital of his *Taiping Tianguo* ('Heavenly Kingdom of Great Peace'), which controlled one-third of China.

THE END OF THE HEAVENLY KINGDOM

Soon after the capture of Nanjing, Hong became a recluse. Without his guidance, the Taiping leadership feuded. Hong spent most of his time with his concubines or meditating. The Qing saw their opportunity and in 1864 they besieged Nanjing, starving the inhabitants. Hong claimed he could live on manna alone and began to eat the weeds growing about the city. On 1 June Hong died, possibly as a result of food poisoning.

On 19 July, the Qing army entered the city. In the ensuing slaughter, at least 100,000 Taiping soldiers and civilians were killed. When Hong's grave was discovered his body was exhumed, then beheaded and burned. The loss of Nanjing spelled the end for the Taiping Rebellion, which quickly withered as the Qing re-established their authority.

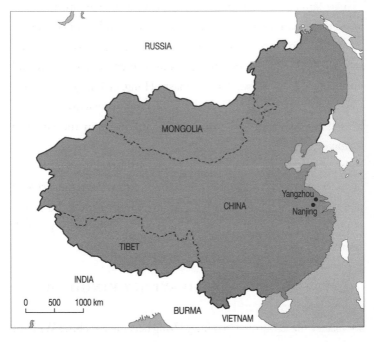

The Qing Dynasty (1644–1912)

LEOPOLD II:
THE NINETEENTH CENTURY'S
MOST BLOODY RULER

Leopold II became King of Belgium in 1865 but achieved infamy for his brutal rule of Congo in Central Africa. Leopold had made frequent visits to the region from 1876, claiming he wanted to carry out humanitarian work. This was merely a front for Leopold's business ambitions, as the area was rich in valuable ivory, minerals and rubber.

In 1885, Leopold set up the Congo Free State, which was a private territory under his control. The people there were subject to the harsh discipline of his personal army and treated as virtual slaves. They were disciplined using the *chicotte*, a whip of raw sun-dried hippo hide cut into a long, sharp-edged corkscrew strip. In the villages, women were held hostage, while men were forced to gather rubber according to strict quotas: 3–4 kilos per adult male per fortnight. If the village refused to comply the inhabitants would be massacred.

Leopold was so eager to save money in his territory that he ordered that each bullet used had to be accounted for. By way of proof, the right hand of each person shot dead was amputated, smoked and presented to Leopold's agents. Leopold built up a huge personal fortune from the Congo but at great cost: under his rule the territory's population dropped from 20 to 10 million. His savage regime continued until 1908, when global outrage at his atrocities prompted the Belgian government to take over the administration of the Congo.

Bibliography

Appian, *Civil Wars* (Loeb Classical Library)

Argenti, Philip P. (ed.), *The Massacres of Chios Described in Contemporary Diplomatic Reports* (John Lane)

Axworthy, Michael, *The Sword of Persia: Nader Shah, from Tribal Warrior to Conquering Tyrant* (I. B. Tauris)

Barlow, Frank, *Thomas Becket* (Weidenfeld and Nicolson)

Bauer, Susan W., *The History of the Ancient World: From the Earliest Accounts to the Fall of Rome* (W. W. Norton)

Baumgartner, Frederic J., *Henry II: King of France 1547–1559* (Duke University Press)

Benedetti, Jean, *Gilles de Rais: The Authentic Bluebeard* (Peter Davies)

Blease, W. Lyon, *Suvarof* (Constable and Co.)

Bores, George, *A True Discourse. Declaring the Damnable Life and Death of One Stubbe Peeter* (Edward Venge)

Brodie, Fawn M., *No Man Knows My History: The Life of Joseph Smith* (Vintage)

Brook, Timothy, Bourgon, Jérôme and Blue, Gregory, *Death by a Thousand Cuts* (Harvard University Press)

Cassius Dio, *The Roman History* (Penguin)

Castel, Albert and Goodrich, Tom, *Bloody Bill Anderson: The Short, Savage Life of a Civil War Guerrilla* (University Press of Kansas)

Cavendish, R. (ed.), *1001 Historic Sites You Must See Before You Die* (Cassell)

Costen, Michael, *The Cathars and the Albigensian Crusade* (Manchester University Press)

Dalley, Jan, *The Black Hole: Money, Myth and Empire* (Penguin)

David, Saul, *The Indian Mutiny 1857* (Viking)

Deakin, Michael A. B., *Hypatia of Alexandria: Mathematician and Martyr* (Prometheus Books)

Diehl, Daniel and Donnelly, Mark, *The Big Book of Pain: Punishment and Torture Through History* (The History Press)

Donnelly, Jr., James S. *The Great Irish Potato Famine* (Sutton)

Dunning, Chester S. L., *A Short History of Russia's First Civil War: The Time of Troubles and the Founding of the Romanov Dynasty* (Pennsylvania State University Press)

Encyclopaedia Britannica

Figes, Orlando, *Crimea: The Last Crusade* (Allen Lane)

Foglietta, Uberto, *The Sieges of Nicosia and Famagusta in Cyprus* (Waterlow and Sons)

Foucault, Michel, *Discipline and Punish: The Birth of the Prison* (Vintage)

Fuchs, Richard L., *An Unerring Fire: The Massacre at Fort Pillow* (Stackpole)

Garraty, John A. and Carnes, Mark C. (eds), *American National Biography* (Oxford University Press)

Gibbon, Edward, *The History of the Decline and Fall of the Roman Empire* (Everyman)

Grant, R. G. (ed.), *1001 Battles that Changed the Course of History* (Cassell)

Guiley, Rosemary Ellen, *The Encyclopaedia of Witches, Witchcraft and Wicca* (3rd Edition, Checkmark)

Haig, Wolseley (ed.) *The Cambridge History of India* (Cambridge University Press)

Harvey, Godfrey Eric, *History of Burma: From the Earliest Times to 10 March 1824* (Cass)

Hemming, John, *The Conquest of the Incas* (Penguin)

Herodian, *History of the Roman Empire* (University of California Press)

Hibbert, Christopher, *George III: A Personal History* (Viking)

Hibbert, Christopher, *The House of Borgia* (Constable)

Hobbins, Daniel (ed.), *The Trial of Joan of Arc* (Harvard University Press)

Hochschild, Adam, *King Leopold's Ghost: A Story of Greed, Terror, and Heroism in Colonial Africa* (Papermac)

Hook, Judith, *The Sack of Rome 1527* (2nd edition, Palgrave Macmillan)

Hough, Richard, *Captain James Cook* (Coronet)

Howgego, Raymond John, *Encyclopaedia of Exploration to 1800* (Hordern House)

Hughes, Lindsey, *Peter the Great: A Biography* (Yale University Press)

Jackson, Peter and Lockhart, Laurence (eds), *The Cambridge History of Iran* (Cambridge University Press)

Jones, A. H. M., *Sparta* (Basil Blackwell)

Kamen, Henry, *Spain in the Later Seventeenth Century, 1665–1700* (Longman)

Kamen, Henry, *The Spanish Inquisition: A Historical Revision* (Yale University Press)

Kozák, Jan and Cermák, Vladimir, *The Illustrated History of Natural Disasters* (Springer)

Lauring, Palle, *A History of the Kingdom of Denmark* (Høst & Søn)

Loomis, Stanley, *Paris in the Terror: June 1793–July 1794* (Jonathan Cape)

Madriaga, Isabel de, *Ivan the Terrible: First Tsar of Russia* (Yale University Press)

Man, John, *Attila the Hun: A Barbarian King and the Fall of Rome* (Bantam)

Matthew, H. C. G. and Harrison, Brian (eds), *Oxford Dictionary of National Biography: From the Earliest Times to the Year 2000* (Oxford University Press)

McGrew, Roderick, *Paul I of Russia 1754–1801* (Clarendon Press)

Muston, Alexis, *The Israel of the Alps: A History of the Waldenses from their Origin to the Present Time* (Griffin Bohn and Company)

The New Catholic Encyclopaedia (2nd edition, Gale)

Noord, Roger van, *King of Beaver Island: The Life and Assassination of James Jesse Strang* (University of Illinois Press)

Olster, David Michael, *The Politics of Usurpation in the Seventh Century: Rhetoric and Revolution in Byzantium* (Adolf M. Hakkert)

Parish, Graeme, *Image of Chile* (Charles Knight & Co)

Parr, Charles McKew, *So Noble A Captain: The Life and Voyages of Ferdinand Magellan* (Robert Hale)

Peretti, Ferdinando, *Julius III and Innocenzo Ciocchi del Monte* (Andreina & Valneo Budai Editori)

Pitts, Vincent J., *Henri IV of France: His Reign and Age* (Johns Hopkins University Press)

Plutarch, *Lives* (Loeb Classical Library)

Polybius, *Histories* (Penguin)

Reid, Robert, *The Peterloo Massacre* (Heinemann)

Reis, João José *Slave Rebellion in Brazil: the Muslim Uprising of 1835 in Bahia* (Johns Hopkins University Press)

Ritter, E. A., *Shaka Zulu: The Rise of the Zulu Empire* (Greenhill Books)

Roberts, Michael, *The Early Vasas: A History of Sweden, 1523–1611* (Cambridge University Press)

Robson, L. L., *A History of Tasmania* (Oxford University Press)

Rosen, William, *Justinian's Flea: Plague, Empire and the Birth of Europe* (Jonathan Cape)

Rothert, Otto A., *The Outlaws of Cave-in-Rock* (Arthur H. Clark)

Runciman, Steven, *A History of the Crusades* (Cambridge University Press)

Runciman, Steven, *The Fall of Constantinople 1453* (Cambridge University Press)

Saunders, J. J., *The History of the Mongol Conquests* (Routledge and Kegan Paul)

Schiff, Stacy, *Cleopatra: A Life* (Virgin)

Scott, Samuel F. and Rothaus, Barry (eds), *Historical Dictionary of the French Revolution, 1789–1799* (Greenwood Press)

Sinor, Denis, *History of Hungary* (George Allen & Unwin)

Somel, Selcuk Aksin, *Historical Dictionary of the Ottoman Empire* (Scarecrow Press)

Spence, Jonathan D., *God's Chinese Son: The Taiping Heavenly Kingdom of Hong Xiuquan* (W. W. Norton & Co.)

Strom, Yale, *The Expulsion of the Jews: 500 Years of Exodus* (SPI Books)

Sturgis, Amy H., *The Trail of Tears and Indian Removal* (Greenwood Press)

Struve, Lynn, *Voices from the Ming-Qing Cataclysm: China in Tigers' Jaws* (Yale University Press)

Stommel, Henry and Stommel, Elizabeth, *Volcano Weather: The Story of 1816, the Year Without a Summer* (Seven Seas)

Spielvogel, Jackson J., *Western Civilization, Volume A: To 1500* (Wadsworth)

Suetonius, *The Twelve Caesars* (Penguin)

Tezcan, Baki, *The Second Ottoman Empire: Political and Social Transformation in the Early Modern World* (Cambridge University Press)

Tighe, Harry, *A Queen of Unrest* (Swan Sonnenschein & Co.)

Treptow, Kurt W. and Popa, Marcel, *Historical Dictionary of Romania* (Scarecrow Press)

Trow, M. J., *Vlad the Impaler: In Search of the Real Dracula* (Sutton)

Wedgwood, C. V., *The Trial of Charles I* (Penguin)

Wedgwood, C. V., *William the Silent: William of Nassau, Prince of Orange 1533–1584* (Phoenix Press)

Wheeler, James Scott, *Cromwell in Ireland* (Gill & Macmillan)

Wilson, Peter H., *Europe's Tragedy: A History of the Thirty Years' War* (Allen Lane)

Witakowski, Witold (ed.), *Pseudo-Dionysius of Tel-Mahre Chronicle Part III* (Liverpool University Press)

Wood, Frances, *The First Emperor of China* (Profile Books)

Wooding, Lucy, *Henry VIII* (Routledge)

Wyatt, David K., *History of Thailand* (Yale University Press)

Zamoyski, Adam, *1812: Napoleon's Fatal March on Moscow* (Harper Perennial)

Index

(page numbers in italics refer to illustrations)